AIR VANGUARD 23

MESSERSCHMITT Bf 109 E–F SERIES

ROBERT JACKSON

First published in Great Britain in 2015 by Osprey Publishing,
PO Box 883, Oxford, OX1 9PL, UK
PO Box 3985, New York, NY 10185-3985, USA
E-mail: info@ospreypublishing.com

Osprey Publishing, part of Bloomsbury Publishing Plc

© 2015 Osprey Publishing Ltd.

All rights reserved. Apart from any fair dealing for the purpose of private study, research, criticism or review, as permitted under the Copyright, Designs and Patents Act, 1988, no part of this publication may be reproduced, stored in a retrieval system, or transmitted in any form or by any means, electronic, electrical, chemical, mechanical, optical, photocopying, recording or otherwise, without the prior written permission of the copyright owner. Enquiries should be addressed to the Publishers.

A CIP catalogue record for this book is available from the British Library

Print ISBN: 978 1 4728 0489 1
PDF ebook ISBN: 978 1 4728 0490 7
ePub ebook ISBN: 978 1 4728 0491 4

Index by Rob Munro
Typeset in Sabon
Originated by PDQ Media, Bungay, UK
Printed in China through Worldprint Ltd

15 16 17 18 19   10 9 8 7 6 5 4 3 2 1

Osprey Publishing supports the Woodland Trust, the UK's leading woodland conservation charity. Between 2014 and 2018 our donations are being spent on their Centenary Woods project in the UK.

www.ospreypublishing.com

CONTENTS

INTRODUCTION   4

DESIGN AND DEVELOPMENT   5
- The engine
- Armament

THE BF 109E   7
- Development and sub-variants
- The Twin Wasp 109
- T for Träger

THE BF 109F   12
- Bf 109F sub-variants
- Bf 109F developments

COMPARISON SPECIFICATIONS   18

OPERATIONAL HISTORY   19
- Phoney War
- The Norwegian Campaign
- The Battle of France, May–June 1940
- Battle over Britain
- Attack of the Eagles
- The Bf 109F enters combat
- The Channel Front, 1941–42
- Operation *Barbarossa*
- North Africa and the Mediterranean, 1941–42

ASSESSMENTS   58

CONCLUSION   62

BIBLIOGRAPHY AND FURTHER READING   63

INDEX   64

MESSERSCHMITT Bf 109 E-F SERIES

INTRODUCTION

The combat experience of the early models of the Messerschmitt Bf 109 in Spain and Poland proved beyond all doubt that Messerschmitt had designed a fine fighting machine, and moreover one that had plenty of scope for further development.

The last Bf 109 variant to see combat in Spain, and the first to feature major design changes, was the Bf 109E. The true prototype of the 'Emil' was the Bf 109 V14, D-IRTT, which flew for the first time in the summer of 1938 and which carried an armament of two wing-mounted MG FF cannon and two 7.92mm machine guns installed in the upper decking of the fuselage nose. The Bf 109 V15, D-IPHR, differed in having a single engine-mounted MG FF cannon and no wing guns, while the pre-production Bf 109E-0 was armed with four MG 17 machine guns. The first aircraft were delivered to JG 132 at Düsseldorf in December 1938.

The 'Emil' series eventually extended to the E-9, including models built as fighters, fighter-bombers and reconnaissance aircraft. Nineteen Bf 109E-3s were exported to Bulgaria, 40 to Hungary, two to Japan, 69 to Romania, 16 to Slovakia, 80 to Switzerland, five to the USSR and 73 to Yugoslavia. The two aircraft delivered to Japan were extensively tested and the Allied code-name 'Mike' was later allocated to the Bf 109 when intelligence reports erroneously indicated that the type had entered service with the Imperial Japanese Army Air Force. The fighter misidentified by US intelligence was in fact the Kawasaki Ki-61, which was powered by a licence-built DB 601A engine.

The Bf 109E first saw operational service in the closing weeks of the Spanish Civil War, a conflict in which fuselage art became popular. This example was operated by III./J 88. (Via Martin Goodman)

By any standards, the Bf 109E was an excellent fighter. Its direct fuel injection system, which prevented the engine cutting out under conditions of negative gravity, was a huge asset in combat. With the slotted flaps lowered 20 degrees the take-off run was remarkably short, and as the main wheels were positioned well forward of the centre of gravity, heavy braking was permitted immediately after touchdown, resulting in a short landing run and fast taxiing without fear of the fighter tipping on its nose.

A Bf 109E-3 of the Swiss Air Force. Switzerland was an early customer for the 109, ordering 90 D and E models for 36.6 million francs in 1938. Deliveries were completed in April 1940. (Via Martin Goodman)

However, the tendency of the aircraft to swing during take-off and landing because of its narrow-track undercarriage was something that a pilot had to be ready to counter instantly, and as it could not be cured except by major redesign the problem was never eliminated during the Bf 109's career, even with the introduction of a tailwheel locking device which activated automatically when the throttle was fully opened.

Early in 1940, in order to take full advantage of the increased power provided by more advanced versions of the DB 601 engine, Messerschmitt began refining the Bf 109E in a programme that would result in the best of all Bf 109 variants, the Bf 109F 'Friedrich'. The first production version, the Bf 109F-1, was powered by a 1,200hp DB 601N engine, in which an increase in power at all altitudes had been achieved by switching from the concave-topped pistons of the DB 601A to flat-topped pistons, raising the compression ratio from 6:9 to 7:9. Together with all the improvements, this increase in power resulted in a marked improvement of the Bf 109's performance at all altitudes.

Pre-production Bf 109Fs were evaluated at various Luftwaffe test establishments during the latter months of 1940 and test pilots were enthusiastic about this latest variant, with the result that it was cleared for issue to operational Luftwaffe units in January 1941.

DESIGN AND DEVELOPMENT

The engine

The biggest apparent difference between the Bf 109E and earlier models lay in the engine. Although there was an inevitable weight penalty, with the larger Daimler-Benz DB 601A engine of the Bf 109E being 400lb (181kg) heavier than the earlier Jumo 210, the new engine delivered an extra 300hp, raising the total available horsepower to 1,100. The installation of the DB 601 also required some airframe redesign. Simply enlarging the existing nose-mounted radiator of the Bf 109D would have created more weight and drag, cancelling out the extra power advantage of the new engine, so it was decided to move

This Bf 109D-1, bearing the fuselage code CI+58, is thought to have been one of several aircraft used as a test bed for the Daimler-Benz DB 600 engine, originally intended for the Bf 109E. This example came to grief against a railway embankment following an engine failure. (Via Martin Goodman)

the main radiators to underwing positions, leaving only the oil cooler in a small streamlined duct under the nose. The new radiator position also had the effect of counterbalancing the extra weight and length of the DB 601, which was fitted with a heavier three-blade VDM propeller. To accommodate the new radiators the wings were almost completely redesigned and reinforced, with several inboard ribs behind the spar being cut down to make room for the radiator ducting. Although the cooling system was more efficient than that of the earlier-model 109s, it needed extra ducting and piping, which was susceptible to battle damage. Another danger was that the underwing radiators were potentially vulnerable to becoming clogged by mud and debris when the fighter was taxiing on wet airstrips.

The DB 600-series engines had been designed from the outset to support a 20mm gun fitted in the 'V' formed by the cylinder blocks and which fired through the hollow shaft of the propeller reduction gear. This arrangement produced an unexpected spin-off in that the supercharger had to be repositioned, and it proved impracticable to fit the carburettor to it in the normal way. The designers tried several variations, and in the end they dispensed with the carburettor altogether and instead used a multi-point fuel injection system spraying directly into the cylinders. The result was that the Daimler engine continued to perform well during all combat manoeuvres – unlike the Rolls-Royce Merlin, which tended to cut out because of a negative 'g' effect on the carburettor float chamber when the aircraft was inverted or when the pilot put the nose down to dive on an enemy. The direct fuel injection system was installed in the DB 601A, and was to give the Bf 109E a huge advantage in combat.

Armament

In the early 1930s France led the field in the development of engine-mounted aircraft cannon, and in 1932 the German Air Ministry, which had monitored French progress with interest, issued a requirement for Rheinmetall-Borsig to develop a similar weapon. The resulting gun, designated MG C/30L, was intended to fire through the propeller hub and was large and powerful, but it had a slow rate of fire and trials with the weapon installed in a Heinkel He 112 revealed that it was not suitable for air combat.

Instead, the 20mm cannon selected for the Bf 109E was the drum-fed automatic MG FF, developed in 1936 by the Ikaria Werke Berlin and derived from the Swiss Oerlikon FF. The MG FF (Flügel Fest, or wing mounted) had been tested in early models of the Bf 109 and had encountered many teething problems, but these were progressively corrected and it was selected for mass production. It could be used in fixed or flexible mountings, as an offensive weapon in fighters or a defensive weapon in bombers. Although it had a lower muzzle velocity and slower rate of fire than other contemporary

> **THE HEINKEL He 100**
> The Messerschmitt Bf 109E had one rival for the Luftwaffe production contract. Originally designated He 113, the Heinkel He 100 monoplane fighter was developed as a potential competitor of the Bf 109E. The prototype flew for the first time in January 1938 and proved to be very fast. Despite the fact that subsequent prototypes established a number of speed records the type was not selected for production, the six prototypes and three pre-production aircraft being sold respectively to the USSR and Japan. Twelve production He 100D-1s were in fact built and were exploited by the German propaganda machine, being adorned with false markings to give the Allies the impression that the fighter was in large-scale service. They were used for a time to provide air defence for the Heinkel factory at Rostock.

aircraft cannon, it had the advantage of being lighter and shorter. Wing installation in the Bf 109 was not easy, as the drum required a good deal of space, and as a consequence the ammunition storage was initially reduced to 60 shells per drum, which limited firing time to only about seven seconds. The MG FF had a muzzle velocity of about 600m/sec and a rate of fire of 520 rounds per minute.

In the summer of 1940 the MG FF was adapted to fire a new type of high capacity, high explosive mine shell called the Minengeschoss, which had a thinner casing to permit an increased explosive charge. The projectile was lighter and produced less recoil than the standard 20mm shell, making it necessary to introduce slight modifications to the firing mechanism of the gun, which was now known as the MG FF/M. Muzzle velocity was 700m/sec and rate of fire the same as that of the MG FF.

THE Bf 109E

Development and sub-variants

In the latter half of 1938 the RLM (Ministry of Aviation) ordered a batch of ten pre-production Bf 109Es under the designation Bf 109E-0, these being delivered to JG 132 for evaluation in December. The E-0 was armed with four 7.92mm MG 17 machine guns and the initial production model, the Bf 109E-1, carried a similar

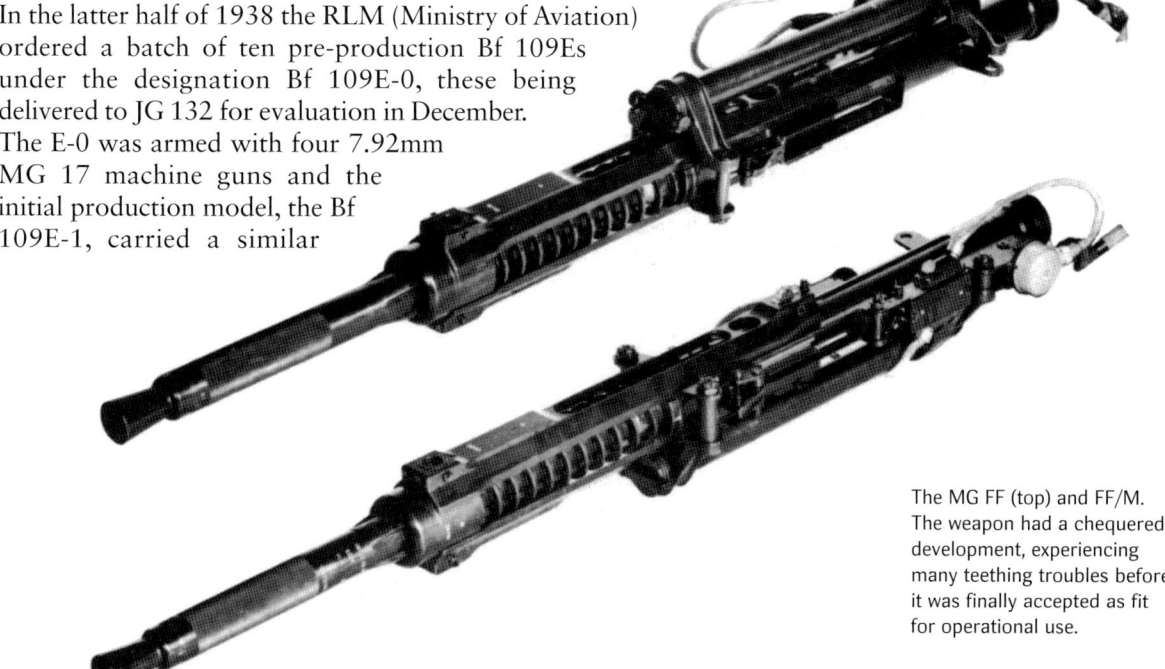

The MG FF (top) and FF/M. The weapon had a chequered development, experiencing many teething troubles before it was finally accepted as fit for operational use.

Messerschmitt Bf 109E-3 fighter being tested in a wind tunnel at the Luftfahrtforschungsanstalt Hermann Göring Aerial Weapon Establishment, one of the leading centres for top-secret aeronautical research, which was on the outskirts of Braunschweig (c.1940). (Bundesarchiv)

armament. It was fitted with the Funkgerät 7 (FuG 7) VHF radio equipment, effective over a range of 30–35 miles (48–56km). The Bf 109E-1/B was a fighter-bomber variant, fitted with racks for 110lb (50kg) SC 50 bombs under the wings or a single 550lb (250kg) SC 250 bomb under the fuselage. This variant used the Bf 109's Revi (Reflexvisier) reflector gunsight as a bomb sight, and the angle of dive was indicated by a red line painted on either side of the cockpit at 45 degrees to the horizon. For bombing from low and medium altitudes the recommended diving speed was 373mph (600km/h), while for high-altitude bombing the recommended diving speed was 403mph (648km/h). The maximum permissible diving speed was 446mph (718km/h). Of the 1,183 Bf 109E-1s built in total, 110 were E-1Bs.

The Bf 109E-2, for which the V20 development aircraft served as the prototype, was produced only in limited numbers. It was armed with two MG FF cannon mounted in the wings and one in the engine, as well as two MG 17 machine guns mounted in the nose.

The Bf 109E-3, which was to be the Allies' principal fighter opponent in the Battle of France, was developed from the V16 and V17 prototypes. It was armed with two nose-mounted MG 17 machine guns and an MG FF cannon in each wing. Total production of the E-3 was 1,267 units, including 83 for export.

By the time the Battle of Britain began in the summer of 1940 the Bf 109E-3

Bf 109E-1
This aircraft was flown by Oberleutnant Karl Fischer of 7./JG 27. It made a forced landing in Windsor Great Park after sustaining battle damage in combat with RAF fighters on 30 September 1940.

Trägergruppe 186 (TGr 186). The Gruppe came into being at Kiel-Holtenau in November 1938, its establishment comprising 4.(Stuka)/186 with Ju 87Bs and 6.(Jagd)/186 with Bf 109Bs, the fighters being transferred from 4./JG 136. A second fighter Staffel, 5.(Jagd)/186, was formed on 15 July 1939 with Bf 109Cs. Both fighter Staffeln were rearmed with the Bf 109E in September–October 1939 and were assigned to the air defence of northern Germany.

Meanwhile, six early model Bf 109s (B and C) and one Bf 109E were modified as trials aircraft for the carrier version, being fitted with catapult attachment points and an arrester hook. The wingspan was increased slightly to 36ft 4in (11.08m). Folding wings were not envisaged. The chord of the ailerons and slats was increased, as was the flap traverse. The conversion work was carried out by Fieseler at Kassel.

Upon successful completion of trials, in particular catapult launches, Fieseler received a contract to build 70 Bf 109T-1s, but after only ten examples had been produced work on the *Graf Zeppelin* was suspended and the remaining 60 aircraft of the order were de-navalised and completed as T-2s. Thanks to the longer wingspan and their modified high-lift devices these aircraft had a shorter take-off and landing run than the standard production Bf 109E, so most were assigned to JG 77 in Norway, where short airstrips that were subject to frequent strong crosswinds made landing and take-off conditions tricky. Powered by a DFB 601N engine, the Bf 109T-2 was armed with two 7.92mm MG 17 guns above the engine and one MG FF/M in each wing.

Work on the *Graf Zeppelin* was resumed for a time in 1942, but by then the Bf 109T was outdated and surviving examples were relegated to training units. In April 1943 some were issued to a newly formed unit, the Jagdstaffel Helgoland, but later in the year they were transferred to Norway, where they remained operational until the summer of 1944.

THE Bf 109F

All the changes made to the Bf 109 airframe in the course of its early development were incorporated in the next variant, the Bf 109F, work on which began in 1939 when Messerschmitt's engineers took two Bf 109E-1 airframes and fitted them with an improved engine, the Daimler-Benz

1: Bf 109E-1 OF 1 STAFFEL, I/JG 20, BRANDENBURG-BRIEST, SEPTEMBER 1940
JG 20 was assigned to the defence of the Reich during the Polish Campaign. The wavy line on the rear fuselage shows that this is the Group Commander's aircraft.

2: Bf 109E-3 OF 4./JG 77, KRISTIANSAND, NORWAY, APRIL 1940
The skeleton on a scythe is chasing the umbrella of the then British Prime Minister, Neville Chamberlain, soon to be replaced by Winston Churchill.

3: Bf 109E-4/B OF ERPROBUNGSGRUPPE 210, CALAIS-MARCK, AUGUST 1940
Armed with a mix of Bf 109s and Bf 110s, EGr 210 carried out low-level precision attacks on shipping and airfields in the Battle of Britain.

4: Bf 109E-7, I./JG 27, AIN-EL-GAZALA, APRIL 1941
The Gruppe at this time was commanded by Major Eduard Neumann, and its pilots included Hans-Joachim Marseille, who was to become the top-scoring fighter pilot of the North African campaign.

1

2

3

4

DB 601E. These two aircraft (Werknummer 5602 and 1800, designated V21 and V22 respectively) retained the E-1's wing planform, but the span was reduced by 2ft (61cm). This was found to have an adverse effect on the aircraft's handling, so another E-1 (V23, Werknummer 5603, factory code CE+BP) was fitted with new rounded (semi-elliptical) wingtips. These were also fitted to a fourth aircraft (V24, Werknummer 5604, factory code VK+AB), which also featured a modified air intake and a deeper oil cooler bath under the engine cowling, which was redesigned to be smoother and more rounded so that the propeller spinner, adapted from that fitted to the new twin-engine Messerschmitt Me 210, blended into it smoothly.

The Bf 109F was equipped with a new three-blade, light alloy VDM propeller unit with a diameter of 9ft 8½in (3m), a little less than that of the Bf 109E. Propeller pitch was changed electrically and regulated by a constant-speed unit, although a manual override was still provided. Thanks to the improved aerodynamics, the more fuel-efficient DB 601E and the introduction of light-alloy drop tanks, the Bf 109F's range was increased to 1,060 miles (1,700km), compared to the Bf 109E's maximum range of 746 miles (1,200km).

The most obvious change to the Bf 109's wing planform in the 109F was the rounded wingtips, which could be removed. The leading edge slats were also redesigned, being made shorter with a slightly increased chord. Frise-type ailerons (a design in which the nose portion projected ahead of the hinge line, so that when the trailing edge of the aileron moved up, the nose projected below the wing's lower surface and produced some parasite drag, decreasing the amount of adverse yaw) replaced the plain ailerons of earlier models. The wing radiators were made shallower and placed farther back, and a new cooling system was introduced. A boundary layer duct allowed continual airflow to pass through the aerofoil above the radiator ducting and exit from the trailing edge of the upper split flap. The lower split flap was mechanically linked to the central 'main' flap, while the upper split flap and forward bath lip position were regulated via a thermostatic valve which automatically positioned the flaps for maximum cooling effectiveness. In 1941 cutoff valves were introduced which allowed the pilot to shut down either wing radiator in the event of one being damaged; this allowed the remaining coolant to be preserved and the damaged aircraft to be recovered to its base.

The fourth prototype Bf 109F (aircraft V24 in the development series (VK+AB), Werknummer 5604) originally flew with clipped wings but featured the modified 'elbow-shaped' supercharger that was adopted for production and a deeper oil cooler bath beneath the cowling. (Via Martin Goodman)

14

The Bf 109F's tail unit underwent some redesign, the rudder being slightly reduced in area and the fin changed to an aerofoil shape, producing a sideways lift force that pushed the tail slightly to the left and reduced the need to apply strong right rudder on take-off in order to counteract the swing for which the earlier 109 models had become notorious. The tailplane was moved to a new position, slightly lower and forward than its position on the Bf 109E, and the conspicuous bracing struts were deleted. A semi-retractable tailwheel was fitted and the main undercarriage legs were raked forward by 6 degrees to improve ground handling.

Production of the new DB 601E engine was slow, so the pre-production Bf 109F-0 and the first series production 109F-1/2 were fitted with the 1,175hp DB 601N. The first production aircraft differed only in their armament, the F-1 carrying an engine-mounted 20mm MG FF/M Motorkanone, with 60 rounds, in addition to its two MG 17 machine guns, with 500 rounds per gun, while in the F-2 the Motorkanone was replaced by the faster-firing 15mm Mauser MG 151, with 200 rounds of ammunition. The first of 208 Bf 109F-1s was issued to Jagdgeschwader 51 at St Inglevert, in the Pas-de-Calais, early in October 1940, and the type was flown operationally by experienced pilots such as Werner Mölders in the later stages of the Battle of Britain.

A fine shot of a Bf 109F turning above the clouds. The aircraft, an F-2, is on a test flight. (Via Martin Goodman)

Bf 109F sub-variants

Bf 109F-0. Pre-production aircraft, assembled from modified Bf 109E airframes. The F-0 was the only F-variant to have a rectangular supercharger intake.

Bf 109F-1. The first to be fitted with the 1,159hp DB 601N engine driving a VDM 9-11207 propeller. It was armed with a 20mm MG FF/M Motorkanone with 60 rounds, firing through the engine hub, and two synchronized engine-mounted 7.92mm machine guns. The F-1 saw some action in the Battle of Britain in October 1940, with JG 51. Production was 208 aircraft, built between August 1940 and February 1941 by Messerschmitt Regensburg and the Wiener Neustädter Flugzeugwerke (WNF).

Bf 109F-2. The Bf 109F-2 introduced the Mauser MG 151 Motorkanone with 200 rounds, supplemented by two synchronized engine-mounted 7.92mm MG 17 machine guns with 500 rounds per gun. Production of the F-2, which was shared by AGO Flugzeugwerke, Arado, Erla, Messerschmitt Regensburg and WNF, ran to 1,380 aircraft. No tropicalized version of the F-2 was built, but individual aircraft were retrofitted with sand filters for service in North Africa and were known as F-2/Trop. The F-2/Z was to have been a high-altitude interceptor with GM-1 boost, but was cancelled.

Bf 109F-3. This sub-variant was fitted with the 1,332hp DB 601E engine, which had broader propeller blades to improve altitude performance. Armament was the same as that of the F-1. Only 15 examples of the F-3 were produced before production gave way to the F-4.

Bf 109F-4. Production of the F-4, armed with the new 20mm Mauser MG 151/20, reached a total of 1,841 aircraft. The type was first issued to first-line units in June 1941. Some late production aircraft were armed with two 20mm MG 151/20 cannon in faired underwing gondolas, with 135 rounds per gun, and were designated F-4/R1. Production was 240 aircraft, all built by WNF in the first three months of 1942. A high-altitude interceptor variant, with GM-1 boost and designated F-4/Z, saw extensive use; 544 examples were built, also in the first quarter of 1942. Finally, the Erla factory produced 576 examples of the tropicalized F-4 (trop) in the first half of 1942. A reconnaissance version of the F-4, the F-5, was proposed, but only one example was built. The Bf 109F-4/B was fitted with an under-fuselage rack to carry a 550lb (250kg) SC 250 bomb. Many experimental versions of the Bf 109F were produced, including one (c/n 14003) with a butterfly tail, another with a BMW 801 radial engine for comparative trials with the Focke-Wulf Fw 190, one with boundary layer fences in place of the leading edge slats, and one with a tricycle undercarriage for trials in connection with the Me 262 jet fighter development programme.

Bf 109F developments

Bf 109X

One Bf 109F (D-ITXP, Werknummer 5608) was fitted with a BMW 801 radial engine and was known as the Bf 109X. The airframe differed from that of the standard Bf 109F in that the forward fuselage had a wider cross-section, and the elliptical wingtips were deleted. The Bf 109X first flew on 2 September 1940, with Fritz Wendel at the controls, and despite problems with the BMW 801A engine a test programme went ahead until early 1942, when further development was abandoned.

Bf 109F-1 OF JG 51
This was flown by Major Werner Mölders in the final phase of the Battle of Britain. The aircraft still bears the RLM Stammkennzeichen (Identification Code) SG+GW. The Bf 109F was evaluated during this period by Hauptmann Hermann-Friedrich Joppien, Gruppenkommandeur of I/JG 51.

2: Bf 109F-2 WERKNUMMER 7187, OF I./JG 53, LENINGRAD FRONT, OCTOBER 1941
This aircraft was piloted by Leutnant Fritz Dinger. Dinger was credited with 67 victories before being killed in an Allied bombing raid at Scalea, Italy, on 27 July 1943.

3: Bf 109F-2 OF III./JG 53, RUSSIA 1941
This Bf 109 was flown by Hauptmann Wolf-Dietrich Wilcke, Gruppenkommandeur of III.JG/53.

4: Bf 109F-4 OF 10.(JABO)/JG 26
This Bf 109 was forced down during a fighter-bomber attack and used by No 1426 (Enemy Aircraft) Flight to give demonstrations. It was allocated the RAF serial NN644 and repainted in RAF green-grey camouflage, although the white number 11 and bomb symbol were retained.

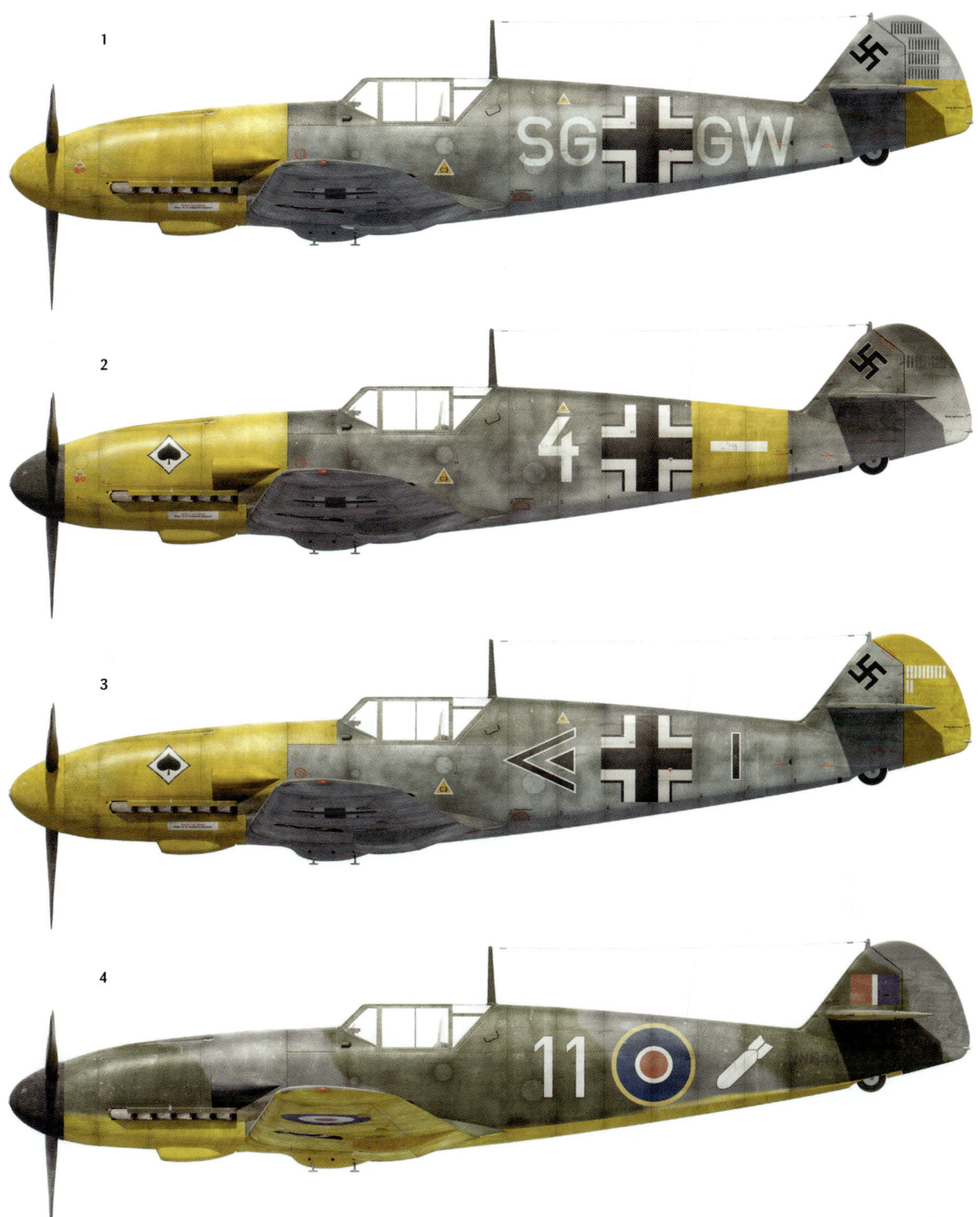

Bf 109Z

The Bf 109Z Zwilling (Twin), of which one prototype was built late in 1942, comprised two Bf 109F airframes joined together by means of a new wing centre section and a new tailplane, both of constant chord, in much the same way as the later North American F-82 Twin Mustang. The pilot sat in the port fuselage, the cockpit in the starboard fuselage being faired over. The Z-1 interceptor version was designed to carry a very heavy armament of five MK 108 30mm cannon, while the Z-2, a fighter-bomber variant, was to have carried up to two 2,200lb (1,000kg) bombs, its built-in armament being reduced to two 30mm MK 108s. The Z-1 and Z-2 were to have been powered by a pair of DB 605 engines, while two more projected variants, the Z-3 and Z-4, were to have been fitted with the Junkers Jumo 213. The span of the Bf 109Z was 43ft 6.5in (13.27m) and loaded weight 13,200lb (6,000kg). The sole completed prototype was damaged in its hangar during an Allied bombing raid in 1943 and never flew.

Luftwaffe pilots who flew the Bf 109F were very enthusiastic about the new variant, but about a month after the first aircraft were issued three early production machines were lost in unexplained circumstances. In each case, radio messages from the pilots indicated that the engine had begun to vibrate violently, followed by a loss of control. A few weeks later, the tail of a Bf 109F-1 broke off in mid-air, and it was discovered that all the bolts in the fuselage/tail assembly joints had been torn out. A thorough inspection of the engine, which had suffered only minor damage in the crash, revealed no technical problems, and suspicion fell on the tail spar, since the rivets between the ribs were all loose, missing or broken. After an exhaustive investigation, it was discovered that when the bracing struts that were a feature of the Bf 109E were deleted on the Bf 109F, the rigidity of the whole tail unit was compromised, resulting in a frequency of oscillation which at certain rpm was overlapped by engine vibration. It was the resultant sympathetic vibrations that had torn out the tail spars. All Bf 109Fs issued to operational units so far were temporarily withdrawn while tail modifications were carried out. Initially, two external stiffening plates were screwed on to each side of the rear fuselage, the whole tail structure being reinforced later on.

COMPARISON SPECIFICATIONS

Messerschmitt Bf 109E-4	
Type	single-seat fighter
Powerplant	one 1,175hp Daimler-Benz DB 601Aa 12-cylinder inverted-Vee engine
Armament	two 20mm fixed forward-firing cannon in leading edges of wing, and two 7.92mm fixed forward-firing machine guns in upper part of forward fuselage
Performance	
Max speed	560km/h (348mph) at sea level
Time to height	7 minutes 45 seconds to 6,000m (19,685ft)
Service ceiling	10,500m (34,450ft)
Max range	660km (410 miles)
Dimensions	
Wing span	9.87m (32ft 4.5in)
Length	8.64m (28ft 4.5in)
Height	2.50m (8ft 2.33in)
Weights	
Empty	2,125kg (4,685lb)
Max take-off	2,510kg (5,534lb)

Messerschmitt Bf 109F-2	
Type	single-seat fighter
Powerplant	one 1200hp Daimler-Benz DB 601E 12-cylinder inverted-Vee engine
Armament	one 15mm fixed forward-firing cannon in an engine installation, and two 7.92mm fixed forward-firing machine guns in upper part of forward fuselage
Performance	
Max speed	600km/h (373mph) at sea level
Max speed	max speed 5 minutes 12 seconds to 5,000m (16,405ft)
Service ceiling	11,000m (36,090ft)
Max range	880km (547 miles)
Dimensions	
Wing span	8.94m (29ft 3.88in)
Length	9.92m (32ft 6.5in)
Height	2.60m (8ft 6.33in)
Weights	
Empty	2,353kg (5,188lb)
Max take-off	3,066kg (6,760lb)

Messerschmitt Bf 109G-6	
Type	single-seat fighter
Powerplant	one 1474hp Daimler-Benz DB 605AM 12-cylinder inverted-Vee engine
Armament	one 20mm or 30mm fixed forward-firing cannon in an engine installation, and two 12.7mm (0.50in) fixed forward-firing MGs in the upper part of the forward fuselage, plus an external bomb load of 250kg (551lb)
Performance	
Max speed	621km/h (386mph) at sea level
Time to height:	6 minutes to 6,100m (20,000ft)
Service ceiling	11,550m (37,890ft)
Max range	1,000km (620 miles)
Dimensions	
Wing span	9.92m (32ft 6in)
Length	8.85m (29ft 0in)
Height	2.50m (8ft 2in)
Weights	
Empty	2,673kg (5,893lb)
Max take-off	3,400kg (7,496lb)

OPERATIONAL HISTORY

On 4 September 1939, the day after Great Britain declared war on Germany following the latter's invasion of Poland, the Royal Air Force launched the first of its attacks against Germany, its targets being units of the German fleet at Wilhelmshaven and in the Elbe Estuary. Five Bristol Blenheims and one Vickers Wellington were shot down by flak, and another Wellington was destroyed by Unteroffizier Alfred Held of II./JG 77, whose Nordholz-based Bf 109Es were assigned to the defence of north-west Germany and the north German harbours. It was the Luftwaffe's first victory against the RAF. In the wake of these costly attacks the RAF suspended offensive operations against Germany for several weeks, restricting its activities to leaflet dropping and reconnaissance. Beginning on 20 September, Bristol Blenheims of No 2 Group RAF made 37 reconnaissance flights over north-west Germany and the northern ports; five Blenheims failed to return, at least some falling victim to Bf 109s.

On 3 December, 24 Wellingtons set out to attack German warships in the Heligoland Bight. Despite being attacked by Bf 109s, all the bombers returned to base. On 12 December, 12 Wellingtons attempting to attack enemy cruisers off the Jade Estuary were intercepted by Bf 109s of II./JG 77 and five were shot down, a sixth crash-landing in England. Despite this disaster, further daylight attacks on German naval forces were authorized, and on 18 December, 24 Wellingtons were dispatched with orders to patrol the Schillig Roads, Wilhelmshaven and the Jade Estuary and to attack any warships sighted. The bombers were detected by two experimental German Freya radar stations on Heligoland and Wangerooge, and soon afterwards they were attacked by Bf 109s and Bf 110s of JG 26, JG 77 and ZG 76. Twelve Wellingtons were shot down, six of them by the Bf 109s of 10./JG 26. This unit, based on Jever, had been formed in September 1939 as a night-fighter Gruppe, a task for which the Bf 109 was completely unsuited, leading to its reversion to the day-fighter role on 9 December. Its encounter with the Wellingtons cost it one Messerschmitt.

An assessment of this disastrous operation by RAF Bomber Command established that some of the bombers had caught fire very quickly after being hit, and as a result priority was given to the fitting of self-sealing fuel tanks to the RAF's Wellington force. Following the raid, daylight armed reconnaissance missions in the Heligoland Bight area were suspended and emphasis placed on the development of night bombing techniques.

'MACKI' STEINHOFF

The six Bf 109s of 10./JG 26, led by Oberleutnant Johannes 'Macki' Steinhoff, were the first to intercept the Wellingtons. The 26-year-old pilot had originally joined the German Navy in 1934, but had transferred to the Luftwaffe in 1936. His leadership talents were such that, only three days later, he had risen to the position of group commander. Steinhoff and his wingman, Corporal Hailmayr, each made two beam attacks on individual Wellingtons. Both bombers fell in flames. For 'Macki' Steinhoff, it was the first success on a road that would end, 167 victories and five and a half years later, in the blazing wreckage of a Messerschmitt Me 262 jet fighter – an accident he would remarkably survive, although at the cost of terrible disfigurement. He would later become Chief of Staff of the post-war Luftwaffe, and Chairman of NATO's Military Committee.

Phoney War

The stalemate that existed on the Western Front between September 1939 and May 1940 became known as the 'Phoney War' because of the lack of activity on the ground, but for the aircrews who faced each other the term was a misnomer. From the very first week of the war, Allied and German fighters skirmished over the Maginot Line on an almost daily basis, except when the state of the weather precluded such encounters, as each side did its best to shoot down the other's reconnaissance aircraft.

On 8 September 1939, French fighters – Curtiss Hawks of Groupe de Chasse (GC) II/4 – engaged Bf 109s for the first time and two of the French

D **Bf 109F-2 OF III./JG 54, KOTLY, RUSSIA, SEPTEMBER 1941**
This Bf 109, 'White 2', was flown by Oberleutnant Max-Hellmuth Ostermann. 33 kill markings are displayed on the rudder.

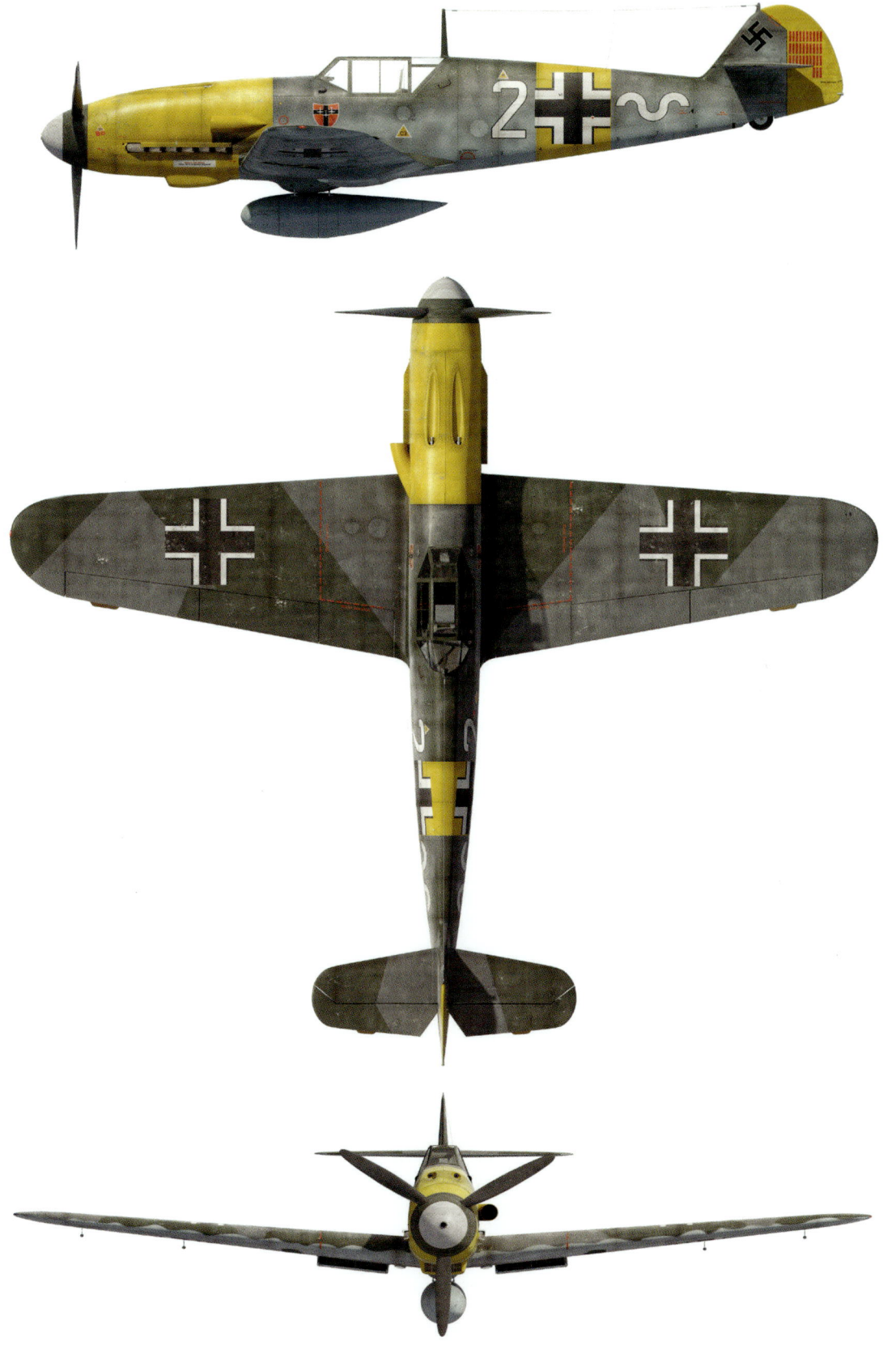

The crews of the lightly armed French Potez 63 reconnaissance aircraft continued to fly missions over western Germany despite suffering terrible losses, and had to be heavily escorted whenever fighters were available. (ECP Armees)

pilots, Adjudant Villey and Sergent-Chef Casenobe, each claimed a Bf 109 destroyed. On 20 September, three RAF Fairey Battle light bombers of No 88 Squadron, Advanced Air Striking Force (AASF), were attacked by Bf 109s near Aachen and two Battles were shot down. The gunner of the third Battle, Sergeant F. Letchford, shot down a 109 – the first enemy aircraft to be destroyed by the RAF in World War II.

The 'Phoney War' period witnessed the rise of Germany's leading air aces. At the forefront was Werner Mölders, who during the Spanish Civil War had developed the air fighting tactics that now gave the Luftwaffe's fighter pilots a huge advantage over their opponents. The outbreak of World War II found Mölders in command of III./JG 53, and it was not long before the unit was in action. On 20 September, six Curtiss Hawks of GC II/5 were escorting a reconnaissance aircraft over the front line when the top flight of three fighters was attacked by four Bf 109s, led by Mölders. The Frenchmen broke away, but they were too late. Mölders got on the tail of a Curtiss and sent it down on fire; the pilot baled out. In the air battle that followed a second Curtiss went down, while the French pilots accounted for a 109.

There were several air combats on 24 September, most of them inconclusive, but in the afternoon there was a fierce battle when six Curtiss Hawks of GC II/4, escorting a Potez 63 reconnaissance aircraft, ran into 15 Bf 109Ds of the Düsseldorf-based I./ZG 52. After damaging a 109, Sergent de la Chapelle was shot down, although he baled out unhurt. In the ensuing dogfight two more 109s were destroyed by adjudants Plubeau and Dardaine; one crashed at Niedergailbach and its pilot, Oberleutnant Borth, was captured by French troops.

The air battles reached their peak of intensity on 30 September, when the French fighter pilots claimed the destruction of 12 Bf 109s and two Henschel Hs 126 observation aircraft for the loss of five of their own number. The most savage fight of the day occurred in the afternoon over the front line, when five Curtiss Hawks of GC I/5 and II/5 were attacked by nine Bf 109s. The Messerschmitts shot down two Hawks on their first pass and then, joined by six more 109s, went after the others. They shot down and killed Sergent Magenz, but two of them were destroyed by Adjudant Genty and two more by Lieutenant Huvet, while a fifth fell to the guns of Sergent-Chef Lachaux.

On this day, four out of five Fairey Battles of No 150 Squadron were shot down by eight Bf 109s while making a reconnaissance of the Saarbrücken area; after that, the AASF's Battles were withdrawn from daylight operations for the time being.

On 22 November 1939, the French fighters flew their largest number of sorties so far – 203 – and claimed a Do 17, probably destroyed by the Morane 406s of GC III/2 over Cambrai, a Heinkel 111 destroyed near Torhout in Belgium by Curtiss Hawks of I/4 and Hurricanes of the RAF's Air Component, and a Do 17 shot down over Mooswald by four Morane 406s of GC II/7. The French lost one fighter, a Curtiss Hawk of GC II/4, shot down at Phalsbourg by a Bf 109 flown by Oberleutnant Helmut Wick of III./JG 2. In the course of the day the French captured a Bf 109 virtually intact when, having suffered battle damage, it landed on Strasbourg-Neuhof airfield. Two more 109s of the same unit (JG 51) were shot down by Allied anti-aircraft fire, while another two were forced to make emergency landings behind their own lines after a fight with six Morane 406s of GC I/3.

So far, the RAF's fighter squadrons in France – four armed with Hawker Hurricanes and two with Gloster Gladiators – had not had the opportunity to meet the Bf 109 in the ongoing aerial skirmishes, most of which took place over the Saar, a long way to the south of where the British fighters were located. During the early weeks of the war the Hurricane squadrons had enjoyed considerable success against lone Heinkel He 111 and Dornier Do 17 reconnaissance aircraft, but on 22 December 1939 three Hurricanes of No 73 Squadron, patrolling the front line, were attacked by five Bf 109s of III./JG 53, which dived on them from high altitude, and two were shot down – one by Werner Mölders and the other by Oberleutnant Hans von Hahn, Staffelkapitän of 8./JG 53 – with the loss of both pilots.

The New Year of 1940 brought an early success for the French fighters. On 3 January they flew 107 sorties, and pilots of GC II/7 claimed a Bf 109 destroyed and a second Bf 109 probably destroyed, together with a Dornier 17. A week later, on 10 January, 15 Curtiss Hawks of GC II/5 destroyed two more 109s; a third Messerschmitt caught fire in the middle of the dogfight for no apparent reason and crashed near Kurtzenhausen. The pilot, Oberfeldwebel Balka, was seriously hurt when he struck the tail unit on baling out. A fourth 109 was destroyed that day by the gunner of a Potez 63 of GR II/55, but the French aircraft was itself shot down by five more 109s of I./JG 54.

Air operations in February 1940 were seriously curtailed by bad weather, and the wiser unit commanders on both sides, aware that the tempo would increase considerably with the onset of spring, took advantage of the respite to send as many of their personnel as possible on leave. They returned, at the beginning of March, in time to take part in some of the most hectic air battles of the war so far. On 1 March, six Morane 406s were attacked by 12 Bf 109s of I./JG 53 while escorting a reconnaissance aircraft over Saarbrücken and one of the French pilots was mortally wounded, although he managed to land his aircraft safely in friendly territory. A second French pilot was wounded the next day in a fight over Metz between the Moranes of GC II/3 and the 109s of Werner Mölders' III./JG 53.

As the Messerschmitts began to penetrate more deeply into France, combats between the 109s and the RAF's fighters became more frequent. On 2 March, Flying Officer J. E. ('Cobber') Kain and Sgt D. A. Sewell were patrolling the front line at 20,000ft (6,100m) when anti-aircraft bursts were seen over

Trondheim. On 7 July 1940, by which time the Norwegian campaign was over, II./TrGr 186 was absorbed into JG 77 and renamed III./JG 77.

Bf 109 Victories in the Norwegian Campaign, April–June 1940

12 April

II./JG 77. Hudson I N7258, 233 Sqn. Shot down SW of Kristiansand by Oberlt Carmann while shadowing KMS *Scharnhorst*.

II./JG 77. Hampden I L4099, 44 Sqn. Shot down off Kristiansand.

II./JG 77. Hampden I P1173, 44 Sqn. Shot down off Kristiansand.

II./JG 77. Hampden I L4064, 50 Sqn. Shot down off Kristiansand.

II./JG.77. Hampden I L4073, 50 Sqn. Shot down off Kristiansand.

II./JG 77. Hampden I L4081, 50 Sqn. Shot down off Kristiansand.

II./JG 77. Hampden I L4083, 50 Sqn. Shot down off Kristiansand.

14 April

II./JG 77. Hudson I N7306, 224 Sqn. Shot down off Stavanger by Oberlt Carmann.

24 April

4./JG 77. Hudson I N7285, 220 Sqn. Shot down off Norway by Lt Demes and Oberfw Arnoldy while escorting destroyers.

4./JG 77. Hudson I N7286, 220 Sqn. Shot down off Norway by Lt Demes and Oberfw Arnoldy while escorting destroyers.

5./JG 77. Hudson I N7283, 224 Sqn. Shot down off Haakonshallen, Norway.

30 April

4./JG 77. Blenheim IV L9242, 110 Sqn. Shot down near Stavanger.

4./JG 77. Blenheim IV N6202, 110 Sqn. Shot down near Stavanger.

4./JG 77. Wellington IA P9215, 37 Sqn. Shot down off Stavanger.

1 May

4./JG 77. Hudson I N7278, 269 Sqn. Shot down off Norwegian coast by Lt Schirmbock.

27 May

II./JG 77. Blenheim IV R3624, 254 Sqn. Shot down off Stavanger by Hauptman Lang.

30 May

5./JG 77. Hudson I N7335, 269 Sqn. Shot down off Stavanger by Fw Menge.

11 June

5./JG 77. Hudson I N7361, 269 Sqn. Shot down off Trondheim.

13 June

4./JG 77. Blackburn Skua (either 800 or 803 Sqn FAA)

4./JG 77. Blackburn Skua (either 800 or 803 Sqn FAA)

4./JG 77. Blackburn Skua (either 800 or 803 Sqn FAA)

4./JG 77. Blackburn Skua (either 800 or 803 Sqn FAA)

4./JG 77. Blackburn Skua (either 800 or 803 Sqn FAA)

(Note: Three more Skuas were shot down by Bf 110s of I./ZG 76. Fifteen Skuas in all were attempting to attack the battlecruiser KMS *Scharnhorst* at Trondheim.)

15 June

5./JG 77. Hudson I N7217, 224 Sqn. Shot down off Stavanger.

5./JG 77. Blenheim IV L9480, 254 Sqn. Shot down off Smøla Island, Trondheim, by Lieutenant Bender.

21 June

II./JG 77. Beaufort I L4486, 42 Sqn. Shot down off Bergen.

II./JG 77. Beaufort I L4501, 42 Sqn. Shot down off Bergen.

II./JG 77. Beaufort I L9810, 42 Sqn. Shot down off Bergen.

5./JG 77. Hudson I N7246, 233 Sqn. Shot down off Utsira, Haugaland.

4./JG 77. Blenheim IV R3826, 254 Sqn. Shot down off Stavanger by Oberfeldwbl Jakob Arnoldy.

25 June

4./JG 77. Blenheim IV N3604, 254 Sqn. Shot down off Stavanger by Oberfeldwbl Jakob Arnoldy.

4./JG 77. Blenheim IV R3622, 254 Sqn. Shot down off Stavanger by Oberfeldwbl Jakob Arnoldy.

27 June

5./JG 77. Hudson I N7330, 269 Sqn. Shot down off Lister, Vest-Agder, Norway.

The Battle of France, May–June 1940

Jagdwaffe (Bf 109 units) Order of Battle in the West and Norway, 10 May 1940.

Luftflotte 1

Unit	Aircraft	Base	Establishment (Aircraft)	Actual strength
Stab II./JG 3	Bf 109E	Döberitz	49	39
Stab JG 1	Bf 109E	Jever	4	4
I./JG 1	Bf 109E	Gymnich	not known	not known
II.(J) TrGr 186	Bf 109E	Wangerooge	48	32
II./JG 2	Bf 109E	Nordholz	47	35
10.(N) JG 2	Bf 109D	Hopsten	31	30
I.(J)/ LG 2	Bf 109E	Wyk auf Föhr	32	22
1 Staffel, I.(J)/LG 2	Bf 109E	Esbjerg	16	10
III./JG 3	Bf 109E	Hopsten	37	25
I./JG 20	Bf 109E	Bönninghardt	48	36
I./JG 21	Bf 109E	Münster	33	31
Stab II./JG 26	Bf 109E	Dortmund	51	39
I./JG 26	Bf 109E	Bönninghardt	44	35
III./JG 26	Bf 109E	Essen-Mülheim	42	22
II./JG 27	Bf 109E	Bönninghardt	43	33
Stab JG 51	Bf 109E	Bönninghardt	4	3
I./JG 51	Bf 109E	Krefeld	47	28

Luftflotte 3

Unit	Aircraft	Base	Establishment (Aircraft)	Actual strength
I./JG 3	Bf 109E	Vogelsang	48	38
Stab JG 77	Bf 109E	Peppenhoven	4	3
I./JG 77	Bf 109E	Odendorf	46	28
II./JG 51	Bf 109E	Böblingen	42	30
Stab JG/52	Bf 109E	Mannheim	3	3
I./JG 52	Bf 109E	Lachen	46	33
II./JG 52	Bf 109E	Speyer	42	28
Stab I./JG 54	Bf 109E	Böblingen	46	31
Stab I/ and III./JG 2	Bf 109E	Rebstock	91	48
III./JG 52	Bf 109E	Sandhofen	48	39
JG 53	Bf 109E	Erbenheim	139	107
I./JG 76	Bf 109E	Ober-Olm	46	37

Luftflotte 5

Unit	Aircraft	Base	Establishment (Aircraft)	Actual strength
4./JG 77	Bf 109E	Sola	12	8
11.(N)/JG 2	Bf 109D	Vaernes	11	6
5. and 6./JG 77	Bf 109E	Kjevik	28	20

Between dawn and dusk on 10 May 1940, during the initial phase of the German assault on France and the Low Countries, the Luftwaffe flew more than 1,000 individual bombing sorties in the course of some 150 attacks. During the morning, 400 Heinkel He 111s, Dornier Do 17s and Junkers Ju 88s struck at 72 air bases, 47 of them in northern France, in an attempt to wipe out a substantial portion of the Allied air forces on the ground. In fact, the Luftwaffe failed to achieve more than a fraction of its objectives during this opening phase; in France's Northern Zone of Air Operations (ZOAN) only four Allied aircraft were destroyed on the ground during the initial onslaught and 30 or so damaged, while in the Eastern Zone (ZOAE) the only real result was obtained by the Dornier Do 17s of KG 2, which destroyed five Amiot 145 bombers and two RAF Hurricanes. Far greater destruction would be wrought on 11 May, when the German bombers caught considerable numbers of Allied machines refuelling and rearming on their bases between sorties.

This Bf 109E, unit unknown, displays a number of victory bars on its rudder. The bars are in the form of horizontal stripes, which were soon changed to smaller vertical stripes. (Via Martin Goodman)

Bf 109Es of I.(J)/LG 2, the Luftwaffe's fighter-bomber Gruppe in the Battle of France. The aircraft nearest the camera carries the so-called Spanienkreuz aft of the Balkenkreuz; this was introduced after the Polish campaign by Hauptmann Harro Harder, who had previously commanded I./J 88 in Spain. Note that the swastika has been deleted from this photo. (Via Martin Goodman)

Belgium's small air force was quickly overwhelmed, mostly in attacks on its airfields. By nightfall on 10 May Belgian losses in the air and on the ground were 53 aircraft, almost one-third of the Belgian Air Force's first-line strength. The Belgians fought on tenaciously with their surviving equipment, much of it obsolescent. The most numerous type was the Fairey Fox, which equipped the majority of the reconnaissance and bomber-reconnaissance units as well as one fighter escadrille. They were supplemented by 13 recently acquired Fairey Battles.

Luftwaffe fighter operations over the Netherlands were mainly the responsibility of JG 20 and JG 26, providing cover for General Fedor von Bock's Army Group B. Their main fighter opponent was the Fiat CR.42, which – although it could hold its own against the Bf 109 in one-versus-one combat – was always faced with superior numbers. In one action on 15 May, Bf 109s accounted for eight out of nine CR.42s that were escorting a formation of Fairey Foxes for the loss of a single 109. By this time the Belgian Air Force had to all intents and purposes ceased to exist, its few surviving aircraft being withdrawn to northern France.

Luftwaffe operations over north-east France during this phase were primarily the responsibility of Fliegerkorps II and V, commanded by lieutenant-generals Bruno Lörzer and Robert Ritter von Greim. The attack on targets in Holland and Belgium was carried out by Fliegerkorps I and IV under generals Ulrich Grauert and Alfred Keller, although part of Fliegerkorps I also participated in attacks on French airfields. In addition, there was Lieutenant-General Wolfram Freiherr von Richthofen's famous Fliegerkorps VIII, whose Stukageschwader had operated with such devastating effect in Poland; the Stukas were now assigned to the direct support of General Walther von Reichenau's 6th Army and General Erich Hoepner's 16th Panzerkorps.

The fighter element of Fliegerkorps VIII was JG 27, a composite unit made up of I./JG 27, I./JG 1 and I./JG 21. On 11 May, JG 27 was tasked with

providing a fighter umbrella over the vital bridges on the Meuse and Albert Canal, newly captured by the Wehrmacht. In 24 hours the German fighter pilots flew 340 sorties, claiming the destruction of 28 Allied aircraft for the loss of only four of their own number. It was the pilots of JG 27 who, on 12 May, destroyed five out of six Fairey Battle light bombers of No 12 Squadron RAF and seven out of nine Blenheims of No 139 Squadron that attempted to attack the bridges.

By this time the RAF had eight squadrons of Hawker Hurricanes in France, and their numbers were being reinforced by aircraft drawn from the UK-based Hurricane squadrons, but on 13 May Air Chief Marshal Sir Hugh Dowding, Commander-in-Chief of RAF Fighter Command, refused to consider any further demands for more of his precious resources to be sent across the Channel. As it became clear that the principal German attacks were aimed at the capture of the Channel ports, the Hurricane squadrons were given the primary task of providing air cover for the British Expeditionary Force, which meant that few fighters could be spared for bomber escort, with disastrous consequences.

After providing air cover over the Meuse bridges on 12 May, the pilots of JG 27 reverted to their more usual task of escorting the Ju 87s of Fliegerkorps VIII, which were heavily engaged in attacking columns in the Liège sector. The Stuka's vulnerability to fighter attack had been demonstrated on 12 May, when six Curtiss Hawks of GC I/5 pounced on 12 unescorted Ju 87s dive-bombing a French motorized column in the Ardennes and shot down 11 of them in a matter of minutes. The strong Luftwaffe participation in this area was part of the overall German plan to convince the Allies that this was the focal point of the battlefront. On 13 May, however, the full weight of Fliegerkorps II and VIII was suddenly turned on the real pivot of the battle, in support of an armoured thrust and subsequent breakthrough at Sedan by the 19th and 21st Army corps. On 14 May, the bridgeheads in the Sedan area were covered by the Bf 109s of JG 2, JG 53 and JG 77, and the Bf 110s of ZG 76. The fighter pilots had a field day; I./JG 53 alone, led by Hauptmann Lothar von Janson, claimed 39 victories in the course of the day. Five of them were credited to Oberleutnant Hans-Karl Mayer, and three to Leutnant Hans Ohly. In all the German fighters (Bf 109s and Bf 110s) flew 814 sorties on 14 May, claiming the destruction of 89 Allied aircraft. Between them, the fighters and deadly four-barrel 20mm Flakvierling mobile anti-aircraft guns destroyed 39 Fairey Battles and Bristol Blenheims of the RAF's Advanced Air Striking Force, over half the total number dispatched.

On 15 May, the inferiority of the Morane 406 in combat with the Bf 109 was tragically demonstrated when nine Moranes of GC III/7 were attacked by 12 Bf 109s over Mézières. The 109s, using their considerable margin of speed (about 60mph) to good advantage, flew round the Moranes in a circle some 5,000 feet higher up and attacked in pairs, afterwards zooming up to altitude once more. With the 109s' first passes two Moranes went down in flames; neither pilot baled out. More 109s joined the battle and the remaining Moranes soon found themselves attacked by three or four adversaries each. A third French fighter went down and this time the pilot managed to bale out, although seriously wounded. A fourth pilot managed to crash-land his damaged machine on the airfield at Soissons, but it was a total wreck. A fifth pilot, Sergent Deshons, was hit in the head by shell splinters and lost consciousness; when he came to he found that his Morane had made a perfect wheels-up landing in a field.

With the situation desperate, RAF Fighter Command dispatched small numbers of Hurricanes from the UK-based squadrons to reinforce those in France. One pilot who went was Flying Officer (later Wing Commander) Jack Rose of No 32 Squadron, who had a dramatic encounter with a Bf 109 during an attack on a formation of He 111 bombers:

On 19 May, after a few hectic days, I was flying one of a formation of six Hurricanes which had been ordered to patrol between Tournai and Oudenarde, about midway between Lille and Brussels, where we had been told to expect German bombers by ground control. We soon spotted twelve or so Heinkel 111s flying in close formation roughly level with us at 12,000 feet, and after a quick check of the sky for enemy fighters we attacked the German aircraft from astern.

I was positioned to attack the Heinkel on the port flank of the enemy formation and closed very rapidly, firing for a few seconds up to very close range, and as I was about to break away the Heinkel's port engine erupted oil which covered my windscreen, almost completely blocking off my forward vision and making the reflector sight useless. I had a quick look round above and behind and, seeing what I took to be an enemy-free sky, I throttled back, gained a little height to reduce speed and pulled back the cockpit hood. I pulled a handkerchief from my right trouser pocket but I couldn't reach far enough to wipe the front of the windscreen clear without releasing my seat harness, so I had to do that and then set about cleaning the windscreen.

Jack Rose DFC, pictured later in the war when he was commanding No 184 Squadron, whose rocket-firing Hurricane IVs were used to attack German V1 flying bomb sites. (Jack Rose)

As I was doing a speed of somewhere between stalling and cruising, my seat harness undone, more or less standing on the rudder stirrups and half out of the aircraft, concentrating on clearing the windscreen and with no armour plate behind, I suddenly saw tracer fly past and felt strikes on the Hurricane. I was being attacked from the rear by a 109 which had not been in sight a few seconds earlier – probably no German fighter pilot has ever had a more inviting target. At my low speed, immediate evasive action resulted in a spin, and from my point of view this was probably the best thing that could have happened. As I was spinning down I left a long trail of glycol and petrol which must have satisfied my German opponent that he need not waste any further rounds on me.

I switched off the engine as soon as I became aware of the glycol and petrol spewing out, but carried on with the spin until the immediate danger of a second attack seemed over. After I had checked the spin and adjusted the Hurricane to a glide I had to decide whether to leave the aircraft in a hurry or try a landing without engine. Then, slightly to the west and 6–7,000 feet below, I spotted the airfield of Seclin, just south of Lille. The aircraft was still discharging fuel and glycol but it had not caught fire. The fire risk was now greatly reduced as the engine temperature had fallen very considerably, so I decided on a wheels-down landing at Seclin. After a long zig-zag glide approach, still with the tell-tale stream behind, I used the hand pump to lock the undercarriage down and lowered the flaps in the last few seconds before touching down.

Under all the circumstances it was a reasonably good landing...

By 17 May the French day bombers had been virtually eliminated from the battle for the time being, while the RAF's Advanced Air Striking Force had practically ceased to exist. The RAF continued to attack with the UK-based Blenheim squadrons of No 2 Group, and suffered appalling losses. On 17 May, 12 aircraft of No 82 Squadron from Watton in Norfolk were detailed to attack an enemy armoured column near Gembloux, Belgium. A few miles from the target, flying in two formations of six at 8,000ft, they ran into intense and highly accurate anti-aircraft fire which caused them to open out. They were at once attacked by the Bf 109s of I./JG 3, operating from Peppenhoven close to the Belgian border. They destroyed ten of the unescorted Blenheims. An 11th aircraft was shot down by flak. The sole survivor, badly damaged, succeeded in getting back to base.

The Bf 109 Gruppen, supporting the German armoured thrusts towards the Channel coast, had to move quickly as one airstrip after another fell into German hands. For example, I./JG 2, having begun the campaign at Kirchberg, moved to Dockendorf on 13 May, Bastogne on 14 May, Beaulieu-en-Argonne on 18 May, Signy-le-Petit on 20 May and Cambrai on 26 May. It would move six more times before the campaign ended in late June. The immense effort behind the Luftwaffe's logistics organization, created in Spain and refined in Poland, had proved its worth.

From the air support point of view, the Panzers' headlong career towards the coast created some serious problems. On 23 May the Stukageschwader of General Wolfram von Richthofen's Fliegerkorps VIII were based near Saint-Quentin after leapfrogging from one French airstrip to another in the wake of the speeding armour, but even then the Channel ports were at the limit of their radius of action. If the Stukas were to be in a position to give maximum support during the land assault on the ports it was obvious that the air units would have to be moved still further forward; but the ports were within easy reach of the RAF fighter bases in southern England, and von Richthofen was fully aware that if his dive-bombers operated in this area without strong fighter escort they were likely to suffer severe losses.

To ensure at least some protection for the Stukas during this preliminary battle for the ports, it was decided to move I./JG 27, part of the fighter element of Fliegerkorps VIII, to Saint-Omer, which until a few hours earlier had been occupied by units of the Advanced Air Striking Force. On arrival overhead, however, the Messerschmitt pilots saw that a battle was still raging for possession of this airfield, and they were forced to divert to Saint-Pol, where they remained for a week before moving to Guise.

So far, with one exception, the only RAF fighter encountered by the Bf 109 pilots during the Battle of France had been the Hawker Hurricane. The exception was an engagement that took place on 13 May, when six Boulton Paul Defiant fighters of No 264 Squadron RAF, accompanied by six Spitfires of No 66 Squadron, were bounced by Bf 109s over Holland. The Spitfires, scattered by the surprise and ferocity of the attack, were unable to protect the Defiants and five of the latter were shot down. One Spitfire was damaged and made a forced landing, its pilot evading capture.

One of the French fighter types involved in the defence of Paris was the Bloch 151, seen here in Vichy French markings. Its designer, Marcel Bloch, changed his name to Dassault – his French Resistance identity – after the war and was responsible for the famous Mirage series of jet fighters. (ECP Armees)

The Dewoitine D.520, France's finest fighter, came too late to influence the air war over France. It subsequently saw widespread service with the Vichy forces. (Via S. Anable)

It was during the evacuation of Allied troops from Dunkirk that the Bf 109 pilots began to engage significant numbers of Spitfires, beginning on 23 May. In the heat of battle the RAF pilots made some quite outrageous claims, as doubtless did their opponents. No 92 Squadron, for example, claimed to have destroyed 17 Bf 110s and six Bf 109s during a series of patrols between Calais and Dunkirk; the Germans admitted to losing two of each type, while No 92 Squadron lost three Spitfires.

At no time during the Battle of France was the superiority of the Bf 109E over the Hawker Hurricane demonstrated more dramatically than on 7 June, when 11 of the British fighters – six of them from No 43 Squadron – were shot down by Bf 109s during patrols over France. Three of the pilots were killed. This day also saw the loss of Flying Officer 'Cobber' Kain of No 73 Squadron, the RAF's leading ace with 17 victories, who crashed while performing unauthorized aerobatics over the squadron's base at Echmines.

With the British Expeditionary Force driven from France and the French Army in the north shattered, the Germans gathered their strength for the second phase of the campaign, an offensive south of the river Somme. On 3 June, as a preliminary, the Luftwaffe launched Operation *Paula*, a massive bombing attack on industrial targets and airfields in the Paris area. Seven Kampfgeschwader were assigned to the operation, escorted by six Jagdgeschwader – some 500 aircraft in total. The French put up every available fighter – including their latest Dewoitine D.520s, which were belatedly reaching the Escadres de Chasse – but their efforts lacked coordination; there was no early warning system and no real fighter control, and the enemy bombers often arrived over the French airfields before the fighters could take off. During the battle the French shot down 26 enemy aircraft; but 17 French fighters were destroyed in air combat and 16 more on the ground.

The Dewoitines were involved in desperate air battles that took place on 5 June, as the French fighters strove to protect Paris and its environs from further air attacks. At 17.05, six D.520s of GC I/3 were sent out on an air cover mission in the Bray-sur-Somme sector. They were accompanied by eight more D.520s of GC II/7, flying at a higher altitude. At 25,000ft over Compiègne the latter were attacked by 15 Bf 109s of III./JG 53. Twenty-five more enemy fighters circled at a distance, ready to pick off any stragglers. The 109s swept through the French formation in a dive, shooting down two D.520s and badly damaging a third in their first pass. The three pilots of II/7's lower flight turned to meet the attackers head-on and one of them, Sous-Lieutenant Rene Pomier-Layragues, set a 109 on fire and caused its pilot to bale out. The German was none other than III./JG 53's Gruppenkommandeur, Hauptmann Werner Mölders. Taken prisoner by French artillerymen, Mölders asked if he could

E **BATTLE OF BRITAIN**
This plate illustrates the combat that took place on 6 September 1940, between Flt Lt Witold Urbanowicz of No 303 (Polish) Squadron and the Bf 109E-3 (Werknummer 1380) of Hauptmann Joachim Schlichting, commanding III./JG 27. Schlichting's aircraft was shot down at Shoeburyness, Essex. The pilot baled out, badly burned, and was taken prisoner.

This Bf 109E-1 of 5.Staffel, II./JG 52 was damaged in combat with RAF fighters over Hastings on 12 August 1940 and its pilot, Unteroffizier Zaunbrecher, made a forced landing at Mays Farm, Selmeston, Sussex. (Via Martin Goodman)

meet the man who had shot him down. He was too late. Even as the German ace parachuted down, Pomier-Layragues found himself in a desperate single-handed fight with four 109s. He shot one of them down, but then his own aircraft was set on fire, crashing and exploding in the suburbs of Marissel. The pilot did not bale out.

Werner Mölders did not remain a captive for long. On 22 June, the Franco-German Armistice brought hostilities in France to an end.

Battle over Britain

In June 1940, while the Battle of France still raged, the Luftwaffe began to concentrate its fighter units on newly captured French airfields close to the Channel coast, bringing south-east England within range of the Bf 109. To give the fighters a degree of autonomy, the Geschwader were grouped into tactical fighter commands under the control of a Jagdfliegerführer, those in the area of Luftflotte 2 being commanded by Generalmajor Kurt-Bertram von Döring and those in the area of Luftflotte 3 by Oberst Werner Junck. Respectively, the two commands controlled 460 and 300 Bf 109E fighters.

From 5 June, small numbers of unescorted bombers began attacking so-called 'fringe' targets, such as ports, on the English coast, and on 30 June Reichsmarschall Hermann Göring, Commander-in-Chief of the Luftwaffe, issued a general directive setting out the aims of the planned air assault on Britain. The attacks on fringe targets were a prelude to larger-scale attacks, starting early in July, on shipping in the English Channel, the aim being to probe Fighter Command's defences and reaction times, in addition to inflicting physical damage on its fighter squadrons. The convoy attacks continued during July and the first week of August. Although there were several major air battles during this phase, usually in the Dover area, the enemy formations were usually intercepted by only half a dozen British fighters, and were often able to carry out their attack and head for home before any British fighters arrived. One reason for the relatively few British fighters engaged was that Air Chief Marshal Sir Hugh Dowding, AOC-in-C Fighter Command, was husbanding his valuable fighter resources; he had earlier turned down repeated requests to send more RAF fighter squadrons to France, knowing that the decisive battle would be fought over the British Isles. His fighter assets at the beginning of July 1940 numbered about 600 aircraft – 29 squadrons of Hurricanes, 19 of Spitfires, seven of Blenheim fighters (most of which were assigned to night defence) and two of Boulton Paul Defiants. One of the latter squadrons, No 141, lost six aircraft in an encounter with Bf 109s on 19 July, and after that the Defiant played no further part in the daylight phase of the battle.

The air battles of July 1940 cost the Luftflotten 48 Bf 109s destroyed, with a further 14 damaged, although about a third of these losses were attributable to accidents. Seventeen pilots were killed, with 14 missing and 13 wounded. RAF Fighter Command losses were higher, with 27 Hurricanes and 27 Spitfires destroyed in combat, together with the six Defiants mentioned above and four Bristol Blenheim Mk IF fighters. Twenty-three Hurricane and 25 Spitfire pilots were killed. It was a sure indication of the bitter fighting that was to come.

The British Air Defence System

Britain had one major advantage in that it had the benefit of the most advanced command-and-control system of air defence in the world. Dowding's approach to air defence was essentially a scientific one; he believed that Britain's air defences should have the benefit of the very latest technological developments. This was reflected in Fighter Command's operations rooms, linked with one another by an elaborate system of telephone and teleprinter lines to provide an integrated system of control. This enabled fighter aircraft to be passed rapidly from sector to sector and from group to group, wherever they were most needed. It was No 11 Group, in the crucial south-east area of England, that would bear the brunt of the fighting throughout the battle; 29 of Dowding's squadrons were based there, with another 11 in No 12 Group, north of the Thames, and 17 in No 13 Group, covering northern England and Scotland.

Nowhere was modern technology more apparent in Britain's defences than in the use of radar, or radio direction finding (RDF) as it was then known. Developed by Robert Watson-Watt from earlier experiments in thunderstorm detection by the use of radio waves, the use of radar as an integral part of the British air defence system was largely the fruit of Dowding's initiative; he had worked with Watson-Watt in the 1930s and had not been slow to recognize the potential of the new invention. The Germans knew all about the British warning radar system, and the destruction of the radar stations on the south coast of England was recognized as a vital preliminary to the main air offensive against England.

Planning for the offensive was completed by 2 August 1940. Luftflotten 2 and 3 were to attack simultaneously, their main tasks being to bring the RAF's fighters to combat, to destroy their airfields and the coastal radar stations, and to disrupt the RAF's ground organization in southern England. The main air offensive against the British Isles was scheduled to begin on 13 August, but the week leading up to it saw intense air fighting as the Jagdwaffe conducted large-scale fighter sweeps over the Channel area. Thursday 8 August was a black day for Fighter Command, with 13 Hurricanes and seven Spitfires lost. Nine Bf 109s were shot down, although nine more were badly damaged. RAF casualties were even higher on 11 August, with 22 Hurricanes and six Spitfires lost; the Luftwaffe lost 14 Bf 109s in combat.

On Monday 12 August the Luftwaffe launched the first of its planned attacks on Britain's south coast radar stations. One unit in particular was heavily involved in these: Erprobungsgruppe 210, which had been specially formed as a

A Royal Air Force officer examines the emblem of II./JG 51 on a Bf 109 brought down during the Battle of Britain. Designed by fighter ace Josef 'Pips' Priller, the emblem depicts a weeping crow with an umbrella and is intended to represent Neville Chamberlain, Britain's prime minister during the early months of World War II. (Via Martin Goodman)

trials unit for the Messerschmitt Me 210, the planned successor to the Bf 110. When the Me 210's development was beset by numerous problems, Erprobungsgruppe's three Staffeln – two armed with Bf 110s and the other with Bf 109E-1/Bs – were fitted with bomb racks. The Gruppe had already carried out several successful attacks on British coastal convoys, and now it turned its attention to the radar stations. While the Bf 110s of 1 and 2 Staffeln attacked Pevensey and Rye with 1,000lb (543kg) bombs, 3 Staffel's Bf 109s unloaded their 500lb (227kg) bombs on to the station at Dover. All three stations sustained damage, but only one, at Ventnor on the Isle of Wight, was put out of action, and that was attacked by Ju 88s.

Fortunately for Britain's air defences, the Germans, although aware of the importance of the radar system, were unaware of its method of operation, and of its crucial value to the whole British air defence structure. Attacks on radar sites were therefore sporadic and were soon abandoned, the Germans believing that the radar sites' operations rooms were in bomb-proof underground bunkers and were consequently invulnerable. In fact, they were mostly in huts above ground.

Except for the station at Ventnor, those damaged on 12 August were operational again within hours. The attempt to blind Fighter Command had failed.

Attack of the Eagles

The Luftwaffe's assault on Britain, code-named *Adler Angriff* (Eagle Attack), was launched on 13 August 1940, and the first days of the attack soon revealed the strengths and weaknesses of both sides. One aspect already appreciated by RAF fighter pilots was the wisdom of arming their Spitfires and Hurricanes with eight machine guns instead of four, as had originally been intended. At first, the idea was that the eight guns would throw out a large bullet pattern, rather like the pellets from a shotgun cartridge, so that the average pilot would stand some chance of striking the enemy, but experience showed that this was a waste of hitting power and eventually the guns were harmonized so that their bullets converged 250 yards in front of the fighter's nose and then spread out again to a width of a few yards within a distance of 500 yards. In the few seconds available in which to destroy or disable an enemy aircraft, the concentration of eight guns firing 8,000 rounds per minute (or 400 per three-second burst, representing a weight of metal of about 10lb) was frequently enough to knock a fatal hole in the wings, fuselage, tail or engine, assuming that the vital cockpit area was not hit. Against this, a three-second burst from a Bf 109's two Oerlikon MG FF 20mm cannon and two 7.9mm machine guns weighed 18lb. But there was a drawback with the Swiss-designed Oerlikon; when the Germans modified it to make it lighter and faster-firing for use in fighter aircraft, they had to reduce the amount of explosive in the shell's charge, reducing the muzzle velocity (the speed at which the projectile leaves the muzzle of the gun) to 1,800ft per second, compared with the Browning's muzzle velocity of 2,660ft per second. The result was that the cannon shells often exploded on impact, causing surface damage but failing to penetrate to a vital part. The Bf 109E-3, the RAF's principal fighter opponent in the Battle of France, had featured four MG 17 machine guns, two mounted in the nose and two in the wings, and an engine-mounted FF cannon firing through the propeller boss. But

Jagdwaffe (Bf 109 units) Order of Battle for Adlertag, 13 August 1940	
Luftflotte 2 (General Albert Kesselring), HQ Brussels	
Unit	**Base**
I./JG 3	Colembert (Boulogne)
II./JG 3	Wierre-au-Bois (Boulogne)
III./JG 3	Desvres (Boulogne)
I./JG 26	Audembert (Cap Gris Nez)
II./JG 26	Marquise (Cap Gris Nez)
III./JG 26	Caffiers (Pas de Calais)
I./JG 51	Saint-Inglevert (Pas de Calais)
II./JG 51	Marquise-Ouest (Pas de Calais)
III./JG 51	Saint-Omer (Formed from I./JG 20, 4 July 1940)
I./JG 52	Coquelles (Pas de Calais)
II./JG 52	Peuplingues (Pas de Calais)
III./JG 52	Coquelles (Pas de Calais)
I./JG 54	Campagne-lès-Guines (Pas de Calais)
II./JG 54	Hermelinghen (Pas de Calais)
III./JG 54	Guines-Sud (Pas de Calais)
Erprobungsgruppe 210	Calais-Marck (Equipped with a mixture of Bf 109 and Bf 110 fighter bombers for precision attacks on shipping, airfields and radar stations, this unit was originally formed as a trials unit for the Messerschmitt Me 210.)
Luftflotte 3 (General Hugo Sperrle) HQ Paris	
I./JG 2	Beaumont-le-Roger (Normandy)
II./JG 2	Beaumont-le-Roger (Normandy)
III./JG 2	Octeville (Le Havre)
I./JG 27	Plumetot (Normandy)
II./JG 27	Crepon (Caen)
III./JG 27	Carquebut (Sainte-Mère-Église)
I./JG 53	Rennes (Brittany)
II./JG 53	Dinan (Brittany)
III./JG 53	Brest Sud/Poulmic (Brittany)

complaints about this arrangement led to the deletion of the nose-mounted cannon, two Oerlikons being installed in the wings of the Bf 109E-4 variant, which equipped many German fighter units during the Battle of Britain.

It was soon established that the Bf 109E-4 was superior to the Hurricane on virtually every count except manoeuvrability and the British fighter's ability to absorb battle damage, and so Fighter Command adopted tactics whereby, in general, Hurricanes would attack the enemy bombers while Spitfires engaged the German fighter escort. The Spitfire was slightly faster than the Bf 109 and certainly more manoeuvrable, although the Messerschmitt had the

A section of Bf 109E fighters preparing for a sortie from a French airfield in 1940. The aircraft nearest the camera bears the double chevron of a Gruppenkommandeur, and carries many kill markings on its tail. (Via Martin Goodman)

Ground crews and Bf 109s of I.(Jagd)/LG 2 at Saint-Inglevert, Pas-de-Calais, in the summer of 1940. In January 1942 I.(J)/LG 2 became the new I Gruppe, JG 77. The Lehrgeschwader's other Gruppe, II.(Schlacht)/LG 2, was dedicated to ground attack. (Via Martin Goodman)

This Bf 109E of I./JG 2 'Richthofen' was disabled by RAF fighters during an attack on Shoreham airfield on 13 August 1940. Its pilot, Oberleutnant Paul Temme, made a successful belly landing and was taken prisoner. (Via Martin Goodman)

edge at high altitude. However, the early attacks on targets in southern England brought a growing confirmation of the Bf 109E's most serious deficiency: a combat radius far shorter than was necessary to provide effective escort to bomber formations carrying out a heavy and sustained air assault. During the Battle of France, the Messerschmitt units had been able to provide effective air cover over the rapidly advancing German ground forces only by leapfrogging from one forward airstrip to another, and only a highly efficient Luftwaffe support echelon had kept the fighters effectively in action.

A greater endurance and range built into the Bf 109E would have eased tremendously the workload imposed on the Luftwaffe logistics system. What is surprising, given the fact that the Japanese had neatly solved their need for long-range fighter escorts by fitting their Mitsubishi Zero fighters with disposable fuel tanks, was that the Germans did not fit similar tanks, which could be jettisoned just before combat, to their Bf 109s. The answer, no doubt, lay in the Luftwaffe's (or rather Göring's) faith in the twin-engined Messerschmitt Bf 110, which had performed well enough against unescorted bombers in earlier battles but which was outclassed in fighter-versus-fighter combat. In 1939, the Luftwaffe was the only air force in the world which had tried to confront the problem of creating an escort fighter with sufficient range to accompany bombers to distant targets. Göring considered his Bf 110 units to be an elite force, and some of Germany's best pilots were assigned to them. The Bf 110's poor acceleration and wide radius of turn made it no match for the Spitfire, but it was a good 40mph faster than the Hurricane and it carried a formidable nose armament of four 7.92mm machine guns and two 20mm cannon, plus a rearward-firing MG15 machine gun. If a Bf 110 had an opportunity to make a high-speed attack from high level and break off after a single firing pass, it could be very effective; but such opportunities were rare over England, and the Bf 110 squadrons suffered appalling losses. It was the Bf 109, therefore, that bore the brunt of the escort work, and there can be little doubt that its lack of range was a critical factor in the defeat of the Luftwaffe. The Bf 109E never had more than 20 minutes of combat time in which to protect its bombers, and its combat radius would take it only as far as the northern suburbs of London. Had the 109 been able to extend its time in the combat area by another 30 minutes through the use of external fuel tanks, then the consequences for Fighter Command might have been dire.

Fliegerkorps II, in whose operational area most of the Bf 109 units were assembled, proposed to attack military and industrial targets in Greater London, intending to draw in British fighters from bases that lay beyond the range of the Bf 109s and engage them in a battle of attrition. This plan was not accepted because Hitler, at this stage, forbade any attacks in the area of the British capital. A somewhat different strategy was therefore adopted in which the RAF's fighters were to be destroyed in the air and on the ground by concentric attacks moving progressively inland, starting with attacks on airfields within a radius of 90 to 60 miles (150km to 100km) south of London. These attacks would take place over a five-day period and would be followed by a three-day assault on targets that lay between 60 and 30 miles (150km and 50km) from the capital. The assault would be completed with a five-day series of attacks on airfields situated within 30 miles of London, after which it was hoped the invasion could be launched.

However, the whole plan was based on a fundamentally flawed intelligence assessment, which among other things predicted that Fighter Command's strength would rapidly decline once the intensified air battle had started; the excellent British aircraft repair and replacement facilities were totally disregarded. The short endurance of the Bf 109, which together with the long approach over the Channel would substantially curtail its combat time over target, was not mentioned; neither was the obvious fact that the short range of the Bf 109 would determine the range of penetration of the bombers in daylight, leaving many of the fighter airfields and industrial installations farther inland out of reach.

Throughout the battle, it was the Bf 109 that was the main cause of Fighter Command's losses. For example, of the 34 RAF fighters lost in the fierce air fighting of 15 August – the heaviest day of the whole battle – 26 were brought down by Bf 109s. In contrast, the Jagdwaffe lost only nine Bf 109s in combat that day, although 21 twin-engine Bf 110s were destroyed, several in Luftflotte 5's attack on targets in northern England. The Luftwaffe's total loss on 15 August was 71 fighters and bombers. By the end of August, the air fighting during the month had cost the RAF 326 fighters (213 Hurricanes and 113 Spitfires), with a further 44 and 40 damaged respectively; the Luftwaffe's fighter losses were 336 (217 Bf 109s and 119 Bf 110s), with 45 and 40 damaged respectively. Fighter Command had suffered 130 pilots killed, with 106 more wounded; Luftwaffe fighter aircrew losses amounted to 134, of which the crews of the Bf 110s accounted for 80. Another 113 Luftwaffe aircrew had been wounded.

By this time the deadline for the establishment of Luftwaffe air superiority over the planned invasion areas of southern England had passed. Indeed, the Germans never came close to achieving it, mainly because they never had enough single-engined fighters to

On 18 August 1940 Oberleutnant Horst Tietzen, Staffelkapitän of 5./JG 51, became the fourth German fighter pilot to record 20 victories in World War II. He was shot down and killed over the Thames Estuary on the same day. (Via Martin Goodman)

39

This Bf 109E-1 of 7./JG 27 overturned when its pilot, Oberleutnant Karl Fischer, tried to make a forced landing in Windsor Great Park after sustaining battle damage in combat with RAF fighters. (Via Martin Goodman)

Bf 109Es of II./JG 52 at Peuplingues, on the Channel coast, in August 1940. The Gruppe was constantly on the move during this period, being located successively in France, Germany and the Netherlands. (Via Martin Goodman)

do so. It is also worth noting that the RAF always had the edge over the enemy in fighter production, receiving about 200 more fighters per month than the German aircraft industry was producing. RAF Fighter Command's biggest problem was not a shortage of aircraft, but of pilots; during the last ten days of August it lost 126 Spitfire and Hurricane pilots, 60 per cent of whom were experienced men. But the Germans were experiencing a similar problem; the savage battle of attrition over southern England meant that new and inexperienced pilots had to be rushed out of operational training units to fill the gaps in units that were being savaged by the RAF's tenacious resistance.

There is no doubt that the RAF's efforts were aided, at various crucial points, by bad decisions on the part of the German leadership. On 19 August, on the personal orders of Hermann Göring – who was becoming increasingly nervous over the lack of results – the Bf 109 units of Luftflotte 3 were ordered to move to new airfields in the Pas-de-Calais in order to extend their combat radius to the utmost limit, and to fly close escort to the bombers, a move that frittered away their tactical advantage. There was also the failure of the Luftwaffe to pursue its primary aim, which was the destruction of the British fighter airfields; this was influenced by faulty intelligence that appeared to indicate that Fighter Command was on the verge of collapse. The Luftwaffe instead initiated large-scale daylight attacks on London and night attacks on other cities. This move resulted in further attrition to the badly mauled Luftflotten, and on 17 September, two days after the Luftwaffe suffered particularly heavy losses during a massed attack on London, Hitler postponed the planned invasion of Britain.

The beginning of October 1940 saw a change in the Luftwaffe's tactics. Attacks on London and targets in southern England were now made by formations of bomb-carrying Messerschmitts operating at high level. At Göring's instigation, one Staffel of each Bf 109 Geschwader in the Channel coast area now rearmed with either Bf 109E-1/B or Bf 109E-7 and E-8 fighter-bombers, concentrating their efforts on London. On 15 October, a morning

attack on the capital by Bf 109s wrecked the approach to Waterloo station and temporarily closed the railway lines. Factories on the south bank of the Thames were badly hit, and in the evening a major attack wrecked parts of the docks, and Paddington, Victoria, Waterloo and Liverpool Street stations. Civilian casualties were 512 killed, with 11,000 made homeless. The Luftwaffe lost 14 Bf 109s that day – not all of them fighter-bombers; the RAF's loss was 15 Spitfires and Hurricanes. Attacks by the high-flying fighter-bombers, operating in streams or in massed formations, continued for another week, but they never again achieved a result comparable to that of 15 October.

Battle of Britain postscript: an ace's story

While Britain's Air Ministry remained reluctant to publicize the exploits of the leading fighter pilots in the Battle of Britain, the Germans had no such inhibitions. Two names, those of Werner Mölders and Adolf Galland – whose respective number of victories reached 54 and 52 by the end of the battle – were featured constantly in the German propaganda organs. But it was a young fighter pilot who had been one of Mölders' pupils in the 1930s who surpassed both of them.

A forester's son, Helmut Wick had been a poor scholar as a child, constantly playing truant to escape into the woods. His sole ambition, then, had been to follow in his father's footsteps, but in 1936 he joined the new Luftwaffe and, under the instruction of Mölders and other skilled pilots, he soon showed exceptional flying talent. He scored his first kill in November 1939, during the 'Phoney War' period, and when the Battle of France began his score mounted with phenomenal speed. He was aggressive and impetuous, and intensely patriotic. His unit was JG 2 'Richthofen'. At the end of October 1940, Helmut Wick's score stood at 49, and he was itching to catch up with his old instructor, Mölders. At the age of 25, Wick was given command of JG 2, making him the youngest Geschwaderkommodore in the Luftwaffe.

On 6 November he led his Bf 109s on a fighter sweep over the Southampton area of southern England, and a day or two later wrote an account of what happened:

> We met a formation of Hurricanes flying lower than ourselves. Just as I was about to start the attack, I saw something above me and immediately called "Look out, Spitfires ahead." The Spitfires were still far enough away to permit an attack on the lower-flying Hurricanes.
>
> At that moment the Hurricanes made a turn, which proved to be their downfall. We shot down four of this group, one of which fell to me. The remaining Hurricanes turned away but began to climb again, and during the climb I caught one of them flying on the right-hand side of the formation. The Hurricanes then dived steeply. I cannot fully explain my next experience – perhaps I was not quite fit or my nerves were frayed – but after my second Englishman went down, I only wanted to fly home. I still had fuel for a few more minutes of action … I saw three Spitfires coming in from the sea in front of me. I saw them first and caught up with them quickly and the first one went down immediately. Now, I said to myself, we must get them all. If we let them get away they will probably kill some of my comrades tomorrow, now away with them!

The artwork on this Bf 109E of III./JG 54 'Grünherz' depicts a hunter with a brace of Spitfires hanging from his belt. Having enjoyed much success during the Battle of Britain, JG 54 rearmed with the Bf 109F and was transferred to the Eastern Front. (Via Martin Goodman)

the Ju 87 Stukas of VIII Fliegerkorps operating from their Bulgarian bases. As the campaign in Greece progressed and airfields were captured, II. and III./JG 27 moved forward with the Stukas, just as they had done during the Battle of France, and by 26 April their Bf 109s were established at Eleusis, near Athens. They remained there on air defence duties for some weeks after the close of the Greek campaign before returning to the Reich in June. Meanwhile, the Bf 109 formations on Luftflotte IV's Order of Battle – II. and III./JG 77, III./JG 52 and I.(J)/LG 2 – had been assigned to cover the airborne assault on the island of Crete in May, after which they withdrew to their airfields in Romania to rearm with the Bf 109F.

Winter 1940–41, and the war went on. Here, ground crew personnel carry out routine maintenance on a Bf 109 in a copse somewhere in France. (Via Martin Goodman)

The Channel Front, 1941–42

Early in 1941, the RAF went over to the offensive, mounting daylight attacks on targets such as airfields, power stations and stores dumps in occupied France. The small numbers of bombers involved in these so-called 'Circus' operations were heavily escorted by squadrons of Spitfires (and initially Hurricanes). At this time the defence of the German-occupied English Channel area rested on only two Jagdgeschwader, JG 2 'Richthofen' and JG 26 'Schlageter', armed with the Bf 109F-1 and F-2. One of the principal tasks of the Jagdgeschwader in 1941 was the defence of the French Channel ports, where the powerful battlecruisers *Scharnhorst* and *Gneisenau* had taken refuge following a series of successful sorties into the Atlantic. Daylight attacks on the warships cost RAF Bomber and Coastal commands dearly; on 24 July 1941, for example, an attack on Brest by 79 Wellington bombers encountered strong and prolonged German fighter opposition, and ten Wellingtons were lost. At La Pallice, five out of 15 Handley Page Halifaxes were also shot down, and all the rest damaged.

A Bf 109F-4/B equipped with an auxiliary fuel tank sits beside a Messerschmitt Bf 110 at Abbeville early in 1942. Both types provided fighter cover for the Scharnhorst, Gneisenau and Prinz Eugen during the famous 'Channel Dash'. (Via Martin Goodman)

By the end of 1941 the formidable Focke-Wulf Fw 190 had made its first appearance on the Channel Front, equipping a Gruppe of JG 26, but the other Gruppen were still armed with either the Bf 109F-2 or F-4 in February 1942, when the *Scharnhorst*, *Gneisenau* and the heavy cruiser *Prinz Eugen* broke out of the Channel ports and headed for Germany in Operation *Cerberus*, better known as the 'Channel Dash'. To cover the breakout, General Adolf Galland, the General der Jagdflieger, had assembled a force of some 250 fighters, mostly Bf 109Fs, drawn from the two Jagdgeschwader already in the Channel area, JG 1 in the Netherlands and Jagdfliegerschule 5 at Bernay, between Caen and Paris.

The plan called for at least 16 single-seat fighters to be overhead the warships at all times in daylight hours during their dash through the English Channel, which started during the night of 11–12 February 1942. Cover during the night was provided by about 30 Messerschmitt Bf 110s. The Luftwaffe liaison officer on board *Scharnhorst* was Oberst Max Ibel, with Oberst Hentschel acting as fighter controller.

Although the British had been anticipating the breakout for some days, the Germans were aided by bad weather, and when attacks were finally launched against the warships they were uncoordinated and piecemeal. RAF Bomber and Coastal commands sent out 242 sorties, but most crews failed to locate the enemy vessels and only one in six attacked them, with no success. Overhead, in the relative few patches of clear sky, RAF fighters fought savage battles with the Luftwaffe. Total British losses were 42 aircraft, 17 of them fighters. Among the 42 were six Fairey Swordfish of No 825 Squadron, Fleet Air Arm, lost in a gallant attack that earned their leader, Lieutenant Commander Eugene Esmonde, a posthumous Victoria Cross. The Luftwaffe also lost 17 fighters out of a total loss of 22 aircraft. All the German warships reached their home waters, although *Scharnhorst* was damaged by a mine.

Since late 1941, JG 2 and JG 26 had each possessed a Staffel of Bf 109F-4/B fighter-bombers, dedicated to carrying out precision attacks on shipping and targets on England's south coast. Fitted with under-fuselage racks for a single 550lb (250kg) SC 250 bomb, these Staffeln specialized in low-level intruder operations to avoid detection by British radar. Their pilots also used the weather to their advantage whenever possible. Often taking off in poor visibility from their airfields at Abbeville, Ligescourt, Poix or Saint-Omer, they would hug the terrain and head out over the Channel at wavetop height. Favourite targets were the towns of Dover, Brighton, Folkestone, Worthing and Newhaven. JG 2's 10.(Jabo) Staffel, based in the south around Évreux and Caen, concentrated on attacking Channel shipping, while 10.(Jabo)/JG 26,

II./JG 2, whose Bf 109Fs are seen here at Calais-Marck with some civilian onlookers, was deployed briefly to Holland to provide additional air cover during the Channel Dash. (Via Martin Goodman)

Bf 109E-4s of III./JG 52 pictured at Bucharest shortly before the invasion of the Soviet Union. The Gruppe converted to the Bf 109F shortly afterwards. (Via Martin Goodman)

JG 77's Leutnant Johann Pichler, seen here on the right, ended the war with as many as 75 victories (the actual total is uncertain). He survived five years in Soviet captivity and died in 1995, aged 82. (Via Martin Goodman)

Most of the German single-engine fighter units were now armed with the Bf 109F. A notable exception was II.(Schlachtgruppe)/LG 2, which began the offensive from its base at Praszniki in Poland, near the Lithuanian border. Armed with 37 Bf 109E-4/B and 17 Henschel Hs 123 fighter-bombers, it formed part of the ground-attack support for 3 Panzergruppe, and featured in the capture of Minsk in June. Its losses were heavy, and by the end of July it was down to just 14 serviceable aircraft.

The destruction wrought by the Jagdgeschwader on the Soviet Air Force during the first two weeks of the offensive was phenomenal. JG 51 alone, providing a fighter umbrella over 2 Panzergruppe, claimed 69 air combat victories on 22 June, while II./JG 51, whose Bf 109Fs had been fitted with ventral bomb racks, claimed 43 more enemy aircraft in the course of four ground-attack sorties. On 24 June Soviet bombers – mostly Tupolev SB-2s – appeared in strength for the first time, and JG 51 destroyed 57, with 24 more victories over other Russian types bringing its score for the day to 81. Yet the poorly armoured, badly armed and unescorted SB-2s continued to attack the German armoured columns, and suffered appalling losses. On 25 June, JG 51 destroyed 83 bombers, while German light flak accounted for about 30 more. In the north, more waves of bombers attempted to destroy bridges over the Dvina River to slow the advance of 4 Panzergruppe, which was heading north-eastwards for Leningrad. The Panzergruppe's spearheads were covered by the Bf 109Fs of JG 54 Grünherz, and in a day of fierce air battles they shot down 65 Russian aircraft.

In fighter-versus-fighter combat between the Bf 109s and the Russian I-153s and I-16s, many of which had been destroyed on their airfields, the situation was not entirely one-sided. Although the 109 had a distinct speed advantage over the I-153 and I-16, the Russian fighters could outmanoeuvre the German fighter, and engaged in a turning fight whenever possible. When a Russian pilot found himself in danger, his tactic was to pull his aircraft into a tight turn and head for his adversary at full throttle. The tactic usually worked, unnerving the enemy pilot and forcing him to break sharply. During this early period of the air war in the east, there were also many instances of Russian pilots deliberately ramming an enemy aircraft, but contrary to widespread belief this was seldom an act of desperation but rather a coolly thought-out manoeuvre demanding the utmost skill and nerves of steel.

Some curious cows inspecting the wreckage of a MiG-3, one of the hundreds of aircraft destroyed in the initial phase of the Luftwaffe's onslaught on the Soviet Union. (Original source unknown, via Robert Jackson)

During the first weeks of the war, Soviet fighter pilots suffered from a lack of combat experience, poor leadership and the restrictions of outmoded air fighting tactics. In the beginning, there had been a general and completely erroneous belief among many pilots that the speed of modern air combat was such that it permitted no calculated tactics, and that there could be no question of teamwork or of working out a plan of action in advance of combat. Incredibly, the lessons of the Spanish Civil War had not been absorbed. This dangerous assumption was soon rejected by several leading Soviet pilots, notably Aleksandr Pokryshkin, who became to the Soviet Air Force what Werner Mölders had already become to the Luftwaffe, and who developed a set of fighting tactics that would enable the Russian pilots to meet their German counterparts on equal terms, and eventually secure air superiority. Pokryshkin scored 14 kills before the end of 1941, eight of them Bf 109s, all while flying the MiG-3 fighter. He would end the war as Russia's second top-scorer, with 59 confirmed victories.

By the end of July 1941, the Luftwaffe had achieved air superiority on all fronts, although fierce air battles still raged in some sectors. While the German

A Bf 109F of II./JG 54 'Grünherz' in the Russian mud. With its pilots including some of Germany's top-scoring aces, JG 54 carved out a formidable reputation for itself in the skies of the Eastern Front. (Via Martin Goodman)

49

Romania ordered 50 Bf 109Es in December 1939, the first 11 being delivered in 1940 and the remaining 39 a year later. They were operated by Grupul 7 of the Royal Romanian Air Force. (Via Martin Goodman)

armies pushed on towards Moscow in the centre and the Black Sea in the south, Army Group North continued its steady drive towards the Gulf of Finland and Leningrad. In late August 1941, two Stukagruppen – I./St.G 2 and III./St.G 2 – which had been operating in support of Army Group Centre under the command of Major Oskar Dinort, were redeployed to the Leningrad Front for intensive operations against lines of communication between Moscow and Leningrad, coming under the orders of Luftflotte 1. The Stukas were based at Tyrkovo, some 90 miles west of Lake Ilmen. Their fighter support was provided by the Bf 109Fs of Major Hannes Trautloft's JG 54, whose pilots had gained 500 victories by the end of July.

Beginning on 21 September 1941, St.G 2 launched an all-out offensive against heavy units of the Soviet fleet in Kronstadt, whose heavy armament was in action against the German spearheads. Attacking the warships was extremely dangerous, as explained by St.G 2 dive-bomber ace Lieutenant Hans-Ulrich Rudel in his book *Stuka Pilot*:

> After our first sortie our luck with the weather is out. Always a brilliant blue sky and murderous flak. I never again experience anything to compare with it in any place or theatre of war. Our reconnaissance estimates that a hundred AA guns are concentrated in an area of six square miles in the target zone. The flak bursts form a whole cumulus of cloud. If the explosions are more than 10 or 12ft away one cannot hear the flak from the flying aircraft. But we hear no single bursts; rather an incessant tempest of noise like the clap of doomsday. The concentrated zones of flak in the air space begin as soon as we cross the coastal strip which is still in Soviet hands. Then come Oranienbaum and Peterhof; being harbours, very strongly defended. The open water is alive with pontoons, barges, boats and tiny craft, all stiff with flak. The Russians use every possible site for their AA guns. For instance, the mouth of Leningrad harbour is supposed to have been closed to our U-boats by means of huge steel nets suspended from a chain of concrete blocks floating on the surface of the water. Even from these blocks AA guns bark at us.

The flak forced JG 54's Messerschmitts to remain at high altitude, where they fought frequent battles with the fighters of the Baltic Fleet Air Force and the 7th Fighter Air Corps. Between them, these two Soviet formations mustered some 1,900 aircraft, of which about 1,200 – mostly obsolescent types – were directly engaged in the Leningrad sector. The Russians never came close to challenging German air superiority. Between 22 June and 5 December 1941 JG 54 claimed the destruction of 1,078 Russian aircraft for the loss of 46 Bf 109Fs in air combat and one on the ground.

At the other end of the vast battlefront, while the siege of Leningrad settled down into a grim stalemate that would last over two years and cost the lives of a million civilians and 300,000 Russian soldiers, the Jagdwaffe's Order of Battle underwent some changes. In September, I./JG 3 was withdrawn and returned to Germany to rearm with the Bf 109F-4, and in October II./JG 3 turned over its Messerschmitts to III./JG 77 and also returned to Germany to re-form and rearm. III./JG 3 followed suit in November, handing over its Bf 109Fs to JG 51.

In September 1941, I./JG 52 had arrived on the Eastern Front from Holland, joining the other two Gruppen of the Geschwader on bases near the Volga. In October, the Geschwader's strength was augmented by a Croation volunteer unit, 15.(Kroatische)/Jagdgeschwader 52, equipped with a mixture of Bf 109Es and Fs, which was established at Mariupol. The remaining Jagdgeschwader supporting Army Group South, JG 77, had suffered badly in the drive towards the Crimea, and its assets were badly depleted by the time II and III Gruppen assembled at Mariupol in December (I./JG 77 was still in Norway, supporting Army Group North).

From the beginning of Operation *Barbarossa*, the Luftwaffe's staunchest ally in the east was the Royal Romanian Air Force (Aeronautica Regala Romana). The ARR's Grupul 7 Vanatoare (7th Fighter Group) was formed on 1 June 1940 and comprised two squadrons, the 53rd equipped with Hawker Hurricane Mk 1 fighters (12 of which had been supplied in 1939) and the 57th with Bf 109E-3s. Later in the year the 53rd Fighter Squadron and its Hurricanes were assigned to the 5th Fighter Group and more Bf 109E-3s were delivered, enabling two new squadrons (the 56th and 58th) to be formed. All 50 Bf 109Es had been delivered by the end of February 1941, the Romanian pilots having been trained during the winter by German instructors at Pipera, near Bucharest. The Luftwaffe personnel belonged to a newly formed Gruppe, I./JG 28, which was established in Romania and which became III./JG 52 in the summer of 1941, after its training task was completed. The Romanian fighters – which

The Russians were not the only enemy. Here, mechanics are using a locally designed heater to warm up the engine of a Grupul 7 Bf 109E. (Via Martin Goodman)

51

A Grupul 7 Bf 109E preparing to taxi. The Romanian Bf 109s suffered severe losses in the early months of Operation *Barbarossa* and were reinforced by 15 ex-Luftwaffe Bf 109E-7s in mid-1942. (Via Martin Goodman)

also included Heinkel He 112s – operated alongside their German counterparts with considerable success, the 7th Fighter Group receiving 15 ex-Luftwaffe Bf 109E-7s in 1942 as replacement aircraft.

Another foreign Bf 109-equipped unit serving alongside the Luftwaffe was a squadron of Spanish volunteers, formed in Madrid in July 1941 and equipped with a mixture of Bf 109Ds and Es. In October it went to Russia, where it was designated 15.Staffel JG 27 and armed with the Bf 109E-7. It fought on the Moscow Front and claimed 14 enemy aircraft by the end of 1941, losing a similar number of its own. It later received Bf 109F-2s and was attached to JG 51 in the Orel sector.

Jagdwaffe Claims and Losses, Eastern Front, June–December 1941		
Unit	Claims	Losses
I./JG 3	274	34
II./JG 3	507	27
III./JG 3	404	19
II./JG 27	39	4 (June–July 1941)
III./JG 27	223	38
I./JG 51	362	26
II./JG 51	450	22
III./JG 51	438	34
I./JG 52	100	13 (October–December 1941)
II./JG 52	321	46
III./JG 52	541	26
I./JG 53	135	13 (June–August 1941)
II./JG 53	184	16 (June–July 1941)
III./JG 53	373	27 (June–October 1941)
I./JG 54	296	28 (July–December 1941)
II./JG 54	444	24
III./JG 54	286	28 (July–December 1941)
II./JG 77	353	37
III./JG 77	500	24

On 20 February 1942, Junkers Ju 52 transport aircraft launched a major airlift operation to an airstrip at Demyansk, south of Leningrad, to supply 100,000 troops of the German X and XI Army corps, encircled by the Red Army's January offensive. Eight transport Gruppen were eventually involved. At first

the Ju 52s flew in singly at low level, but as losses increased due to Soviet air action, the transports adopted tight formations, with strong fighter escort provided by the Bf 109Fs of III./JG 3 and I./JG 51. The airlift was successful; up to 20 May 1942, when a land corridor to the pocket was opened, the Ju 52s flew in 24,303 tons of supplies – a daily average of 276 tons – to the Demyansk pocket. In addition, five million gallons of petrol and 15,446 replacements were flown in, and 22,093 wounded evacuated. But the Germans lost 262 Ju 52s, many as a result of accidents in the winter conditions.

The success of the Demyansk airlift, albeit at such high cost, was to have a dangerous consequence. It convinced Reichsmarschall Hermann Göring, the Luftwaffe C-in-C, that the Luftwaffe was capable of resupplying the German Sixth Army, trapped at Stalingrad in the winter of 1942–43. The promises he made were empty, and the Sixth Army went down in defeat.

By that time, the Jagdwaffe units in Russia had re-equipped, or were in the process of re-equipping with either the Focke-Wulf Fw 190 or the improved Messerschmitt Bf 109G. The day of the Bf 109F, which had achieved such spectacular combat success in the early months of the campaign, was at an end on the Eastern Front.

North Africa and the Mediterranean, 1941–42

The first Bf 109 unit to deploy to the Mediterranean theatre was I./JG 27 under Hauptmann Eduard (Edu) Neumann, detachments of which were sent to Sicily at the beginning of March 1941 to take part in the air offensive against Malta with its Bf 109E-7 fighter-bombers. In mid-April the whole Gruppe deployed to Gazala, where it came under the orders of Fliegerführer Afrika and embarked on intensive operations in support of General Erwin Rommel's Afrika Korps. In September, the arrival of the first Bf 109F-4/Trop fighters of II./JG 27 in North Africa enabled I Gruppe to return to Germany, one Staffel at a time, to rearm with similar aircraft, its Bf 109E-7s being allocated to Luftwaffe units in Italy and Greece. In December 1941 III./JG 27, also armed with the Bf 109F-4/Trop (having left its Bf 109Es with other units in Russia), also deployed to North Africa, so that the whole Geschwader was now operating in the theatre. By the end of 1941, I and II/JG 27 had claimed 92 victories in North Africa for the loss of 41 Bf 109s.

Jagdgeschwader 27 numbered many aces among its pilots, but one stood out above the others. He was Leutnant Hans-Joachim ('Jochen') Marseille. From his arrival in North Africa with JG 27, a combination of flying skill and superb marksmanship enabled him to achieve a formidable score in a very short time. On 22 February 1942, Marseille was awarded the Ritterkreuz after scoring his 50th victory (he already had eight kills to his credit in Europe) and on 3 June he claimed six Allied aircraft in a combat lasting only 11 minutes. By 16 June his score had reached 101, at which point he was sent home on leave.

On 1 September 1942, shortly after returning to JG 27 after a two-

Bf 109E-7s of 7./JG 27 in Sicily, 1942. The second aircraft is unusual in that it carries the chevron and vertical bar of the Geschwader Stab on the engine cowling, rather than the fuselage. (Via Martin Goodman)

This cleverly camouflaged Bf 109E-4/Trop was the mount of Oberleutnant Werner Schröer of I./JG 27. Schröer gained 61 of his 114 victories over North Africa, making him the second-highest scorer in that theatre after Hans-Joachim Marseille. He survived the war and died in February 1985, aged 66. (Via Martin Goodman)

month leave of absence, Marseille caused a sensation by claiming to have destroyed 17 enemy aircraft, mostly P-40 Kittyhawks, in a single day. Later, this claim was to be the subject of much controversy. It was bitterly contested by the RAF, who stated that Marseille's claim exceeded the total Desert Air Force losses for that day. Yet every one of Marseille's claims on 1 September was confirmed by his wingmen, who noted times and locations. Moreover, the losses of the RAF, Australian and South African fighter squadrons for 1 September, taken together, did in fact exceed the claims of all German fighter pilots by about ten per cent.

During September 1942, Marseille's score rose to 158 enemy aircraft destroyed. On 30 September, returning to his base after an escort mission, his Bf 109F suffered engine trouble and he was compelled to bale out of a cockpit filled with smoke. His body struck the tailplane and he fell to his death, his parachute failing to open.

Some of the heaviest fighting experienced by JG 27 occurred in May and June 1942, when the Afrika Korps launched a fierce assault on the Gazala Line, a series of fortified positions known as 'Brigade Boxes' extending from the

Pilots of JG 27 pictured in Sicily on temporary deployment from North Africa to take part in the air attacks on Malta. (Via Martin Goodman)

54

coast into the desert west of Tobruk. At the start of the battle, on 26 May, the Desert Air Force had 290 serviceable combat aircraft, the Germans and Italians 497. By 31 May the British Commonwealth fighter squadrons had flown 1,500 sorties in the army cooperation task and lost 50 aircraft, around 20 per cent of the fighter force. The Germans lost three Bf 109s and two Ju 87 Stukas. In the second week of June all squadrons of the Desert Air Force were committed to the support of Free French forces holding the fortified position of Bir Hakeim, at the southern end of the Gazala Line, which was under heavy and continual attack by the Stukas of St.G 3, escorted by JG 27. After a gallant nine-day stand the Free French Brigade was evacuated, having suffered very heavy casualties. Its resistance had prevented three German divisions from turning the Allied flank and encircling the Gazala Line, enabling the British Eighth Army to regroup and withdraw into Egypt.

On 20 June, with the Gazala Line broken, the Luftwaffe and Regia Aeronautica launched a massive assault on the defences of Tobruk, the Germans flying 580 sorties and the Italians 177 on this one day. Tobruk fell, but the Axis forces pushed on towards Egypt with severely depleted air cover, aircraft serviceability having suffered greatly as a result of this effort and the earlier one at Bir Hakeim. By this time, the Luftwaffe units were becoming desperately short of fuel and spare parts; at times, JG 27 was down to about a dozen serviceable fighters. Attacks on Rommel's Mediterranean convoys by strike aircraft and submarines based on the strategically vital island of Malta were taking a severe toll.

This Bf 109, whose tail sports 17 kill markings (and a pet dog), was the aircraft of Oberleutnant Franz Schiess, who gained 11 of his 67 victories with Stab JG 53 over Malta. He was shot down and killed in September 1943 by a USAAF P-38 over Ischia. (Via Martin Goodman)

Malta: the Island Fortress

While JG 27 battled with the Desert Air Force for possession of the North

Messerschmitt Bf 109F-4/Z fighter-bombers of 10./JG 53 being bombed-up with 50kg bombs at Gela, Sicily, in readiness for an attack on Malta, 1942. The Staffel moved to Martuba in North Africa in June. (Via Martin Goodman)

55

African sky, fierce air combats raged over Malta. In January 1941, Fliegerkorps VIII arrived in Sicily from Norway with its Ju 87 dive-bombers, and in February it received fighter support in the shape of 7./JG 26 under Hauptmann Joachim Müncheberg. Armed with Bf 109Es, the single Staffel claimed 52 victories over Malta's defending fighters (mostly Hawker Hurricanes) for no loss before being redeployed to Libya in June to support the Afrika Korps. It returned to France in August to rearm with the Bf 109F.

Sitting on the rain-drenched North African airfield of Martuba in January 1943, this captured Bf 109F wears the code of No 4 Squadron South African Air Force. The aircraft's eventual fate is unknown. (Via Martin Goodman)

The bulk of the Luftwaffe units were withdrawn from Sicily in March 1941, to take part in the Balkans campaign and later the invasion of Russia, leaving the Regia Aeronautica to continue the air offensive against Malta. The Luftwaffe returned to Sicily in strength towards the end of the year, its bomber force now comprising the Junkers Ju 88s of Fliegerkorps II, and this time it had considerable fighter support. In January 1942 all three Gruppen of JG 53 were established on the Sicilian airfields, I Gruppe being armed with the Bf 109F-4 and the other two with the Bf 109F-4/Z fighter-bomber. In May 1942, I./JG 53 redeployed to the Russian Front, and in June the other two redeployed respectively to Pantelleria and North Africa; II./JG 53 began to receive the Bf 109G-4 in August, and III./JG 53 also began to re-equip in November. Elements of III./JG 3 also operated over Malta in January and February 1942.

On 11 October 1942, Field Marshal Albert Kesselring, commanding Luftflotte 2 in Sicily, launched a further series of air attacks on Malta. The RAF now had well over 100 Spitfires to defend the island, as well as a fighter operations room and improved radar facilities, and in a 17-day period the Luftwaffe lost 34 Junkers Ju 88 bombers and 12 Messerschmitt Bf 109 fighters destroyed, with many more damaged. The RAF lost 24 Spitfires, with 12 pilots killed; 20 more damaged Spitfires had to make forced landings. A few days later, with the British offensive under way at El Alamein and Field Marshal Erwin Rommel's Afrika Korps desperate for air reinforcements, Kesselring called off the air assault on Malta.

F HANS-JOACHIM MARSEILLE

On 3 June 1942, during the battle for the Gazala Line, Hauptmann Hans-Joachim Marseille led III./JG 27 on a mission to Bit Hakeim, escorting Stukas which were dive-bombing the Free French positions there. The Stukas were attacked by the P-40 Tomahawks of No 5 Squadron, South African Air Force, which had inflicted heavy losses on the dive-bombers during earlier raids.

Together with his wingman, Feldwebel Reiner Pöttger, Marseille dived his Bf 109 into the middle of the South Africans, who, doubtless believing that they were being attacked by a far superior force, immediately formed a defensive circle. Marseille got inside it, turning steeply, and gave a P-40 a short burst. The fighter went down vertically and exploded in the desert. Marseille's tactics were unorthodox; turning continually inside the circle of enemy fighters, keeping his airspeed low, he fired in short, accurate bursts. In less than 12 minutes, he had accounted for five more Tomahawks, all of which were seen to crash by Pöttgen, including this P-40 Tomahawk flown by Captain Robin S. Pare of No 5 Squadron South African Air Force. Pare, an ace with 6 victories, was shot down and killed.

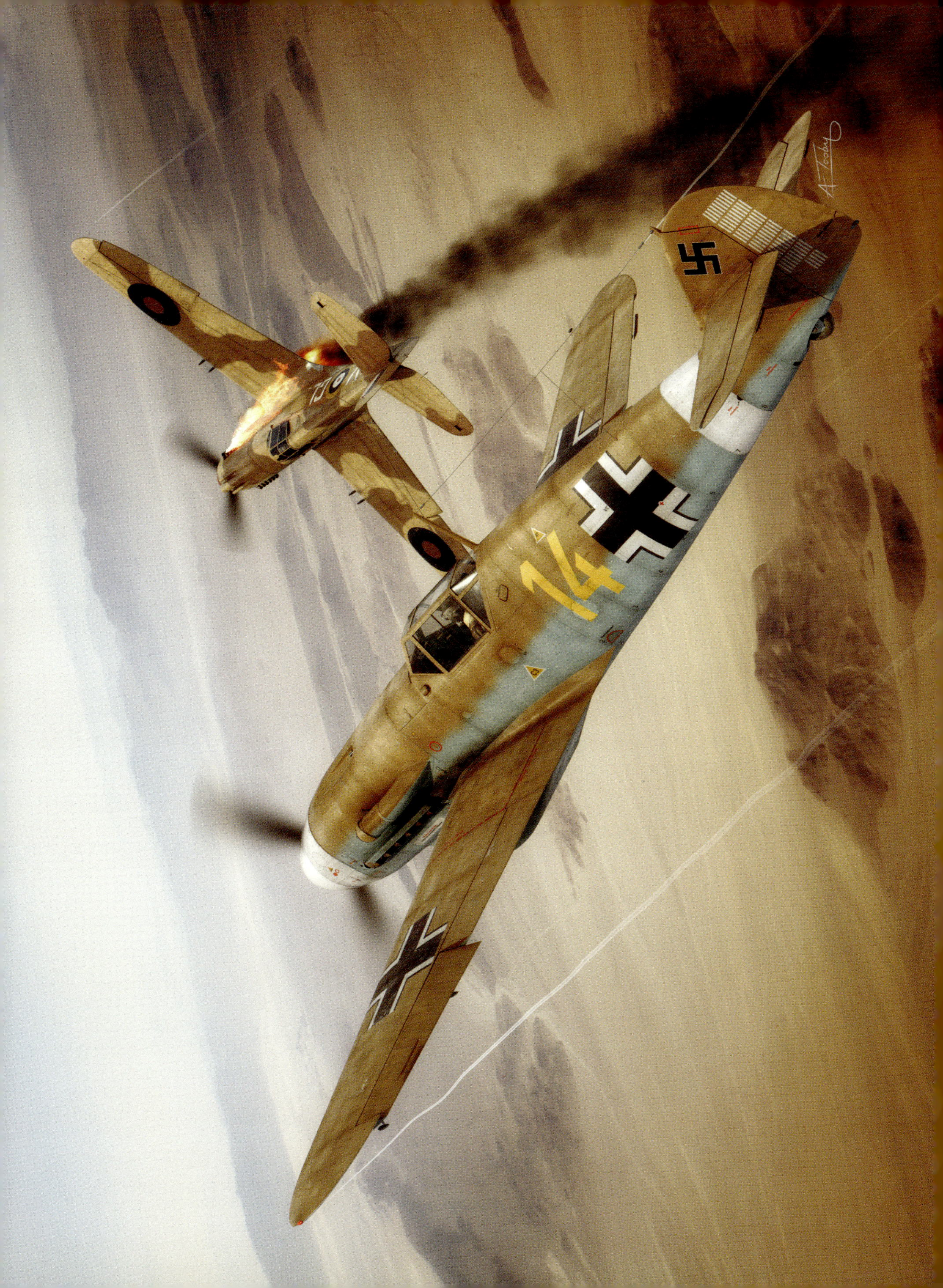
14

This Bf 109E-7/B Trop S9+IS (Werknummer 6431) of 8./ZG 1 crash-landed at Sollum, Egypt on 1 November 1942 after being damaged in combat while covering the retreat of the Afrika Korps from El Alamein. (Via Martin Goodman)

ASSESSMENTS

In the early months of World War II, the Messerschmitt Bf 109E swept all before it in the battle for air superiority over Poland and Scandinavia. During the period of the 'Phoney War', however, it began to encounter much sterner opposition from fighters like the RAF's Hawker Hurricane. On 3 May 1940, only a week before the start of the German Blitzkrieg in western Europe, a Hurricane of No 1 Squadron RAF was flown to Orleans for combat evaluation against a captured Bf 109E-3. This aircraft, Bf 109E-3 Werknummer 1304 of I./JG 76, had landed in error on French territory near Woerth on 22 November 1939.

The Bf 109 (referred to in the report as an M.E. 109) was not fitted with oxygen equipment, so the evaluation was carried out between 10,000ft and 15,000ft. The subsequent report, classified Most Secret, was compiled by Squadron Leader P. J. H. ('Bull') Halahan, commanding No 1 Squadron:

> Both aircraft took off together. Both the take-off and initial climb of the M.E.109 was better than that of the Hurricane, in spite of the fact that the Hurricane was fitted with a Constant Speed airscrew, and full throttle and full revs were used.
>
> At 15,000 feet the aircraft separated and approached one another head-on for the dog-fight. The Hurricane did a quick stall turn followed by a quick vertical turn and found himself on the 109's tail. The pilot of the 109 was unable to prevent this manoeuvre succeeding. From that point the Hurricane pilot had no difficulty in remaining on the tail of the M.E.109. The pilot of the 109 tried all possible manoeuvres and finally the one most usually employed by German pilots, mainly a half-roll and vertical dive. The Hurricane followed this manoeuvre, but the M.E. drew away at the commencement of the dive, and it is felt that had the pilot continued this dive he might have got away. However, in the pull-out the pilot of the M.E. 109 found that it was all that he could do to pull the machine out of the dive at all, as fore and aft it had become very heavy. In fact, the pilot was of the opinion that had he not used the tail adjusting gear, which itself was extremely heavy, he would not have got out of the dive at all.

The pilot of the Hurricane found that he had no difficulty in pulling out of the dive inside the 109, but that he had a tendency to black-out, which was not experienced by the pilot of the 109. This tendency to black-out in the Hurricane when pulling out of high speed dives is in my opinion largely due to the rather vertical position in which the pilot sits. It is very noticeable that in the 109 the position of the pilot is reclining, with his legs well up in front of him. It has been noticed that German pilots do pull their aircraft out of dives at very high speeds, and as I think the position in which the pilot sits is the main reason that black-out is avoided, I feel that this is a point which should be duly considered when in future a fighter is designed to meet other fighters.

After the dog-fight the 109 took position in line astern on the Hurricane and the Hurricane carried out a series of climbing turns and diving turns at high speeds. In the ordinary turns the Hurricane lapped the 109 after four complete circuits, and at no time was the pilot of the 109 able to get his sights on the Hurricane. In the climbing turns, though the 109 could climb faster he could not turn as fast, which enabled the Hurricane again to get round on his tail. In climbing turns after diving, the weight on the elevators and ailerons of the 109 was so great that the pilot was unable to complete the manoeuvre, and in the diving turns he was unable to follow the Hurricane for the same reason.

A fine study of the captured Bf 109E-3, which was allocated the RAF serial AE479 after it arrived in the UK. The aircraft was shipped to the USA in April 1942, but was scrapped following a crash in November that year. (Via Martin Goodman)

> During these tests one point became abundantly clear, namely that the 109, owing to its better camouflage, was very much more difficult to spot from underneath than was the Hurricane. This difference gives the 109 a definite tactical advantage, namely when they are below us they can spot us at long distances, which we when below them find most difficult. As in all our combats at the moment initial surprise is the ideal at which we aim, I strongly recommend that the underside of Hurricanes should be painted a duck-egg blue, the roundels remaining the same, as it is the contrast between black and white only which is so noticeable from below.'

Hurricanes serving with the squadrons of the Advanced Air Striking Force in France had the port wing underside painted black outboard of the wheel well, while the starboard underside was white. This was supposed to serve as a recognition feature, which it did very well, mostly to the advantage of the enemy. Duck-egg blue was soon adopted.

> The M.E. 109 is faster than the Hurricane by some 30 to 40 miles an hour on the straight and level. It can out-climb and initially out-dive the Hurricane. On the other hand it has not the manoeuvrability of the Hurricane, which can turn inside without difficulty. After this clear-cut demonstration of superior manoeuvrability there is no doubt in my mind that provided Hurricanes are not surprised by 109s, that the odds are not more than two to one, and that pilots use their heads, the balance will always be in favour of our aircraft, once the 109s have committed themselves to combat.
>
> In this connection, judging from the tactics at present being employed by the 109s, namely sitting above us and only coming down when they can surprise a straggler, and then only completing one dive attack and climb away, I am fairly certain that the conclusion of the German pilots is the same as our own, and I cannot help feeling that until all Hurricane aircraft have Constant Speed airscrews to enable them to get up to the height at present adopted by the 109s, we shall have few further chances of combat with this particular type of aircraft.

Only three days after Halahan's report was submitted to the Air Ministry, the AASF's Hurricane squadrons would be fighting for their lives against swarms of Bf 109s over the Meuse.

The captured Bf 109 was subsequently flown to England, where it was evaluated against the Spitfire Mk I at the Royal Aircraft Establishment, Farnborough, and the Air Fighting Development Unit at Duxford. RAF pilots who flew it were generally impressed by the aircraft, although most were critical of the cockpit, which they found cramped, with restricted vision to the rear. However, one pilot commented that 'The cockpit enclosure ... excelled among all other aircraft I had flown ... in the complete absence of draught from its clear vision opening. Though rain at times made the windscreen opaque, I could see ahead whatever the speed of the Me 109. In Hurricane or Spitfire it would have been necessary to throttle back and open the hood.'

Pilots also praised the 109's cockpit layout: 'The control column grip came nicely to hand, the single lever, gateless throttle was delightfully straightforward ... the juxtaposition of wheel controls for flap operation and tailplane was excellent.'

Horror stories about the 109's tendency to swing viciously on take-off and drop the left wing were quickly dispelled: 'Response to the throttle was instantaneous ... there was no hasty jamming of rudder to counteract the heavy swing often found with single-engined fighters and the tail lifted firmly and cleanly when the stick was held well forward ... The takeoff was surprisingly short; the aeroplane left the ground sweetly, and slanted up at a rate of climb which would have beaten a competing Spitfire.'

One RAF test pilot who flew the Bf 109 describes a mock combat with a Spitfire:

> The Spitfire ... was alongside with its broad wing tucked between mine and the tail. The pilot grinned and jerked a thumb. I pulled back on the stick, and laughed to see the Spit shoot underneath as the little Messerschmitt stood on its tail and climbed steeply away.
>
> In an endeavour to retrieve his position the Spitfire pilot climbed steeply, but only resulted in placing himself in a position where I could make a short dive for his tail. I jammed the nose down so hard that a Spitfire or Hurricane doing the same manoeuvre would have choked its engine, but the direct-injection system did not even falter. Gun sights could only be held momentarily on the Spitfire; then he did a flick half roll and was off in a steep dive with a change of direction which the Me 109 could not quickly follow.
>
> For a few minutes we climbed, twisted and dived after each other. It was an interesting contest. Many times the steep climbing attitude of the German machine would evade the Spitfire, and the abruptness with which its nose could be thrust down had its undoubted advantage. Yet when it came to manoeuvring at speed ... the heavy weight of the Messerschmitt's controls proved not only exhausting but impossible. Aileron could only be applied slowly, and so the response was slow; the best one could do was to evade the Spitfire by gentle turns at very low speed and then strike him down by cunning. Tighten these turns to 4g and the machine began to drop out of the sky after a preparatory warning flick caused by the opening of the (automatic leading edge) slats. However, the behaviour even then was excellent, for no spin resulted, and normal flight was instantly regained by easing the backward pressure on the stick.

The captured Bf 109F-4 fighter-bomber, previously operated by 10.(Jabo)/JG 26, was almost brand new when it was forced down in England. It is seen here being flown by a Royal Air Force test pilot. (Via Martin Goodman)

CONCLUSION

Although it had been planned to supplant the Bf 109 with the more effective Focke-Wulf Fw 190 early in 1941, technical problems with the latter, in particular with its radial engine, meant that it could not be issued to the Jagdwaffe in substantial numbers until the closing months of the year, and so production of the Bf 109 series was accelerated in the meantime.

The Bf 109F was succeeded by the Bf 109G, which appeared late in 1942. Pre-production Bf 109G-0 aircraft retained the DB 601E of the F series, but the first production model, the Bf 109G-1, had the more powerful DB 605A engine. The G-1, G-3 and G-5 had provision for pressurized cockpits and were fitted with the GM-1 emergency power-boost system, which was lacking in the G-2 and G-4. Various armament combinations were employed, and later aircraft were fitted with wooden tail units. The fastest G model, the Bf 109G-10, without wing armament and with MW 50 power-boost equipment, reached a maximum speed of 687km/h (428mph) at 7,400m (24,250ft), climbed to 6,100m (20,000ft) in six minutes and had an endurance of 55 minutes.

The Bf 109H was intended to be a high-altitude interceptor version of the Bf 109F with an extended span, but was abandoned after only a few had been built because of wing flutter problems. Some were issued to a reconnaissance unit on the Channel coast in April 1944 and made a few reconnaissance flights over the British Isles before the Allied invasion.

The last operational versions of the Bf 109 were the K-4 and K-6, which both had DB 605D engines with MW 50 power boost. The Bf 109K-4 had two 15mm (0.58in) MG 151 guns semi-externally mounted above the engine cowling and a 20mm MK 108 or 30mm Mk 103 firing through the propeller hub. The Bf 109K-6 had the cowling-mounted MG 151s replaced by 12.7mm (0.50in) MG 131 machine guns and had two 30mm MK 103 cannon in underwing gondolas. The last variant was the Bf 109K-14, with a DB-605L engine, but only two examples saw service with JG 52. The Bf 109G was built in both Spain (as the Hispano Ha-1109) and Czechoslovakia (as the Avia S-199). The Spanish aircraft, some re-engined with Rolls-Royce Merlins, served for many years after World War II and some of the Czech-built aircraft were acquired by Israel in 1948, equipping No 101 Squadron of the new Israeli Air Force. In all, Bf 109 production reached a total of approximately 35,000 aircraft.

The Messerschmitt Me 309, first flown in July 1942, was an unsuccessful attempt to provide a successor to the Bf 109. Two prototypes were produced, one being wrecked on its first flight. A further spin-off of the Bf 109 series was the Blohm und Voss Bv 155 high-altitude fighter prototype, whose design was begun by Messerschmitt before the project was transferred to Blohm und Voss. The project was initiated in 1942, soon after reports reached Germany that a high-altitude 'super bomber' – later to materialize as the Boeing B-29 Superfortress – was under development in the United States. Two aircraft were flown early in 1945.

Together with its contemporary and rival, the Supermarine Spitfire, the Messerschmitt Bf 109 was the only single-engined fighter to see operational service from the first day of World War II until the last. Allied pilots who flew captured examples of the Bf 109 in its various incarnations were fairly unanimous in their assessment that the Bf 109F was the finest of the breed. It was a true 'pilot's aeroplane', graceful and aesthetic, and a superlative fighting machine.

BIBLIOGRAPHY AND FURTHER READING

Bekker, Cajus, *The Luftwaffe War Diaries*, Macdonald, London (1967)
Caidin, Martin, *Me 109*, Macdonald, London (1969)
Green, William, *Famous Fighters of the Second World War*, Macdonald, London (1962)
Jackson, Robert, *Air War over France, 1939–40*, Ian Allan, Shepperton (1974)
Jackson, Robert, *Fighter! The Story of Air Combat, 1936–1945*, Arthur Barker, London (1979)
Jackson, Robert, *The Guinness Book of Air Warfare*, Guinness, London (1993)
Jackson, Robert, *The Red Falcons: Soviet Air Force in Action*, Clifton Books, London (1970)
Jackson, Robert, *The World's Greatest Fighters*, Greenwich, London (2001)
Jackson, Robert, *Through the Eyes of the World's Fighter Aces*, Pen & Sword, Sheffield (2007)
Knoke, Heinz, *I Flew for the Führer*, Evans, London (1953)
Nowarra, Heinz J., *The Messerschmitt 109: A Famous German Fighter*, Harleyford, Letchworth (1963)
Royal Air Force Historical Society, *The Battle Re-Thought: A Symposium on the Battle of Britain* (RAF Staff College, June 1990), Airlife, Shrewsbury (1991)
Rudel, Hans-Ulrich, *Stuka Pilot*, George Mann, Maidstone (1973)

INDEX

Figures in **bold** refer to illustrations.

Advanced Air Striking Force (AASF) 22, 23, 29, 30, 31, 60
airfields **B12**, 23, **24**, 25, 28, 29, 30, 31, 32, 34, 35, **37**, **38**, 39, 40, **42**, 43, 44, 45, **46**, 48, **56**
Allies, the 4, 7, 8, **C16**, 18, 20, 23, 24, 25, 27, 29, 31, **46**, 53, 55, 62
armament 4, 6, 8, 15, 16, 18, 19, 38, 50, 62

Battle of Britain 8, **B12**, 15, **C16**, **E32**, 34, **35**, 37, **41**
Battle of France 8, 27, **28**, 31, 32, 34, 36, 38, 41, 44
battlecruisers 26, 44
  Gneisenau **44**; Scharnhorst 26, **44**, 45
Belgium 23, 28, 30
bombers 6, 20, 27, 30, 32, 34, 37, 38, 39, 40, 44, 46, 48, 56
  dive-bombers 11, 31, 46, 50, **F56**; Dornier Do 17 23, 25, 27; Fairey Battle 22, 23, 28, 29; fighter 4, 8, 10, **C16**, 18, **28**, 37, 40, 41, **42**, 45, 46, 48, 53, **55**, 56, **61**; Heinkel 6, 7, 23, 24, 27, 30, 52; He 111 23, 24, 27, 30; He 112 6, 52; Junkers Ju 87B 11, 12; Junkers Ju 88s 27, 36, 56; light 22, 29; Wellington 19, 20, 26, 44
Bulgaria 4, 43, 44

Calais-Marck **B12**, 37, **45**
camouflage **C16**, **54**, 60
cannons 24, 37
  20mm 6, 10, 16, 18, 19, 36, 38; 30mm 18, 19, 62; aircraft 6, 7; forward-firing 18, 19; MG FF 4, 8, 36; shells 24, 36

Dowding, Sir Hugh 29, 34, 35

engines 4, 5, **6**, 8, 11, 12, 15, 18, 19, 24, 30, 36, **51**, 54, 61
  cowling 14, **53**, 62; Daimler-Benz 5, **6**, 12, 18, 19; DB 601A 4, 5, 6, 10, 18; DB 601E 19, 14, 15, 16, 19, 62; DB 601N 5, 10, 15; radial 11, 16, 62; Roll-Royce Merlin 6, 62; single 4, 39, 43, 47, 60, 62; twin 14, 38, 39; Vee 18, 19
English Channel, the 34, 44, 45

fighters 4, 6, 7, **A8**, 11, **B12**, 20, **22**, 23, **24**, 25, 28, 29, 30, **31**, **32**, **34**, **35**, 36, 37, **38**, **39**, **40**, 41, **42**, 43, **44**, 45, 46, 47, 48, 49, 50, 51, 53, 55, **F56**, 58, 59, 60, 62
  bomber 4, **8**, 10, **C16**, 18, **28**, 37, 40, 41, **42**, 45, 46, 48, 53, **55**, 56, **61**; Bristol Blenheim 19, 29, 35; Curtiss Hawks 20, 22, 23, 29; escorts 31, 37, 38, 53; Hawker Hurricanes 23, 24, 25, 27, 29, **30**, 31, 32, 34, 35, 36, 37, 38, 39, 40, 41, 42, 44, 51, 56, 58, 59, 60, 61; Me 262 jet 16, 20; Morane 406 23, 25, 29; pilots **B12**, 22, 25, 29, 30, 36, **39**, 41, 49, 54; single-engined 39, 43, 47, 62; single-seat 18, 19, 45; Spitfire 31, 32, 34, 35, 36, 37, 38, 39, 40, 41, 42, 44, 46, 56, 60, 61, 62; squadrons 23, 34, 54, 55
Fliegerkorps: II 28, 29, 39, 56; VIII 28, 29, 31, 43, 44, 56
Focke-Wulf 16, 44, 46, **47**, 53, 62
  Fw 190 16, 44, 46, **47**, 53, 62
France 6, 23, 24, 25, 27, 28, 29, 30, **32**, 34, **40**, **44**, **46**, **47**, 56, 60
fuselage **4**, **6**, **8**, 18, 24, 36, **53**

forward 16, 18, 19; rear **10**, **B12**, 18; under 16, 45

Gazala Line, the 54, 55, **F56**
Germany 6, 7, 11, 12, 19, 20, **22**, 24, 25, 27, 29, **30**, 31, 32, 34, 35, 36, 37, 38, **39**, **40**, 41, 43, 44, 45, **46**, 47, 48, **49**, 50, 51, 52, 53, 54, 55, 58, 59, 60, 61, 62
Göring, Reichsmarschall Hermann **8**, 34, 38, 40, 53
Great Britain 19, 34, **35**, 36, 40, 41
Groupe de Chasse: GC I/3 23, 32; GC II/4 20, 22, 23; GC II/5 22, 23; GC II/7 23, 32
Grupul 7 **50**, **51**, **52**

Jagdwaffe 25, 27, 35, 37, 39, 43, 46, 47, 51, 52, 53, 62
  Luftflotte: 2 34, 37, 47, 56; 3 27 34, 37, 40; 4 47; 5 27, 39; Jagdgeschwader 32, 44, 45, 48, 51; JG 2 29, 41, 42, 45, **46**, I./JG 1 27, 28; I./JG 2 31, 37, **38**, **47**; II./JG 2 27, 37, **45**; III./JG 2 23, 27; Stab III./JG 2 27, 37; I./JG 3 27, 31, 37, 47, 51, 52; II./JG 3 37, 47, 51, 52; III./JG 3 27, 37, 47, 51, 52, 53, 56; JG 20 **B12**, 28; I./JG 20 **B12**, 27, 37; I./JG 21 27, 28; I./JG 26 20, 28, 44, 45, 46; I./JG 26 27; III./JG 26 27, 37; 10.(JABO)/JG 26 **C16**, 45, **61**; JG 27 28, 29, 53, **54**, 55; I./JG 27 **B12**, 31, 37, 43, 53, **54**; II./JG 27 27, 37, 43, 44, 47, 52, 53; III./JG 27 **E32**, 37, **43**, 44, 47, 52, 53, **F56**; 7./JG 27 **A8**, **40**, 53; Stab JG 27 43, 47; JG 51 15, **C16**, 23, 42, 48, 51, 52; I./JG 51 **C16**, 27, 37, 43, 47, 52, 53; II./JG 51 27, 35, 37, 47, 48, 52; III./JG 51 37, 47, 52; Stab JG 51 27, 47; JG 52 51, 62; Stab JG 52 27, 47; I./JG 52 27, 37, 51, 52; II./JG 52 27, **34**, 37, **40**, 47, 52; III./JG 52 27, 37, 44, 47, **48**, 51, 52; I./JG 53 **C16**, 23, 29, 37, 47, 52, 56; II./JG 53 25, 37, 47, 52, 56; III./JG 53 **C16**, 22, 23, 24, 32, 47, 52, 56; I./JG 54 23, 37, 47, 52; II./JG 54 37, 43, 47, 52; III./JG 54 **D20**, 37, **41**, 47, 52; JG 77 12, 20, 25, 26, 29, **38**, 47, **48**, 51; II./JG 77 19, 20, 25, 26, 43, 47, 52; III./JG 77 26, 43, 44, 47, 51, 52; 4./JG 77 **B12**, 26, 27; 5./JG 77 26, 27; Stab JG 77 27, 43
Japan 4, 7, 38
Jever 20, 25, 27

Kain, Flying Officer J. E. 'Cobber' 23, 24, 32
Kristiansand **B12**, 25, 26

Leningrad 48, 50, 51, 52
Front **C16**, 56
Luftwaffe 5, 7, 11, 18, 19, 20, 22, 27, **28**, 29, 31, 32, 34, 35, 36, 38, 39, 40, 41, 43, 45, 46, 47, **49**, 51, **52**, 53, 55, 56

machine guns 15, 36, 42
  7.92mm 4, 15, 38; forward-firing 18, 19; MG 17 4, 7, 8, 15, 36
Malta 53, **54**, **55**, 56
manoeuvres 49, 58, 59, 61
Marseille, Leutnant Hans-Joachim **B12**, 53, **54**, **F56**
Mediterranean, the 46, 53, 55
Messerschmitt 4, 5, 6, **8**, 12, 15, 18, 20, 22, 23, **24**, 25, 31, 35, 37, 38, 40, 42, **44**, 45, 46, **47**, 50, 51, 53, **55**, 56, 58, 61, 62
  Bf 109 4, 11, **D20**, 22, 23, **24**, 25, 26, 27, 28, 29, 30, 31, 34, **35**, 36, 37, 38, 39, 40,

42, 43, **44**, 46, 52, 53, **55**, **F56**, 58, 60, 61, 62; Bf 109D 5, 22, 27, 52; Bf 109E **4**, 5, **6**, 7, **11**, 12, 14, 15, 18, 19, 25, 27, **28**, 32, 34, **37**, **38**, **40**, **41**, 43, 47, **50**, **51**, **52**, 53, 56, 58; Bf 109E-0 4, 7; Bf 109E-1 7, **A8**, **B12**, **34**, **40**, **42**; Bf 109E-1/B 8, 36, 40; Bf 109E-3 4, **5**, **8**, **B12**, **E32**, 36, 51, 58, **59**; Bf 109E-4 10, 18, 37, **48**, **54**; Bf 109E-4/B **B12**, 48; Bf 109E-7 10, **B12**, 40, **52**, **53**; Bf 109E-7/B **58**; Bf 109E-8 10, 40; Bf 109F 5, 12, **14**, **15**, **C16**, 18, **41**, 42, **43**, 44, **45**, 46, 47, **48**, **49**, 50, 51, 53, 54, **56**, 62; Bf 109F-1 5, 15, **C16**, 18, 42, 44; Bf 109F-2 15, **C16**, 19, **D20**, 44, 52; Bf 109F-4 **C16**, **44**, 45, **47**, 51, 56, **61**; Bf 109F-4/B 16, **44**, 45; Bf 109F-4/Z 16, **55**, 56; Bf 109G 46, 53, 62; Bf 110 10, **B12**, 20, **24**, 25, 26, 29, 32, 36, 37, 38, 39, **44**, 45, 46; Me 109 58, 60; Me 210 14, 24, 35, 36, 37
Metz 23, 24, 25
Mölders, Werner 15, **C16**, 22, 23, 25, 32, 34, 41, 42, 49
muzzle velocity 6, 7, 36

Netherlands, the/Holland 28, 31, **40**, 45, 51
North Africa **B12**, 16, 43, 53, **54**, **55**, **56**
Norway **B12**, 25, 26, 27, 47, 56
Norwegian Campaign, the **24**, 25, 26

operations: Barbarossa 46, 47, 51, **52**; Paula 32

Paris **31**, 32, 37, 45
Pas-de-Calais 15, **38**, 40
Phoney War, the 20, 22, 41, 58
Poland 4, 19, 25, 28, 31, 48, 58

radiators 5, 6, 14
reconnaissance 10, 16, 23, 25, 28, 50
  aircraft 4, 20, **22**, 23, 24; bomber 28; flights 19, 62; missions 62; Potez 63 reconnaissance aircraft **22**, 23; unit 62
RLM (Ministry of Aviation) 7, 11, **C16**
Romania 4, 43, 44, 47, **50**, **51**, **52**
Rommel, General Erwin 53, 55, 56
Royal Air Force (RAF) **A8**, **C16**, 19, 20, 22, 24, 25, 27, 29, 30, 31, 32, **34**, **35**, **38**, 39, **40**, 42, **43**, 44, 45, 54, 56, 58, **59**, 60, **61**
  Bomber Command 20; Fighter Command 29, 34, 35, 36, 37, 38, 39, 40; No 2 Group 19, 30; squadrons: No 1 24, 25, 58; No 12 29; No 32 30; No 43 32; No 66 31; No 73 23, 24, 32; No 82 30; No 88 22; No 92 32; No 139 29; No 145 42; No 150 23; No 184 **30**; No 264 31; No 603 42; No 825 45
Russia/Soviet Union/USSR 4, 7, **C16**, **D20**, 48, **49**, 50, **51**, 52, 53, 56

Saint-Omer 31, 37, 45
shells: 20mm 7; Minengeschoss explosive 7, 10; splinters 29
Sicily 53, **54**, **55**, 56
Sola 25, 27, 47
Spain 4, 25, **28**, 31, 52, 62
Spanish Civil War, the **4**, 22, 49
Staffeln 12, 36, 45
  1 36; 2 36; 3 36; 4 25; 5 25; 6 25
Stavanger 25, 26, 47

World War II 22, 24, **35**, **39**, 58, 62

64